Kh

Afghan Women, Media and Emerging Democracy

Social Evolution in Post-Taliban Afghanistan

VDM Verlag Dr. Müller

Impressum/Imprint (nur für Deutschland/ only for Germany)

Bibliografische Information der Deutschen Nationalbibliothek: Die Deutsche Nationalbibliothek verzeichnet diese Publikation in der Deutschen Nationalbibliografie; detaillierte bibliografische Daten sind im Internet über http://dnb.d-nb.de abrufbar.

Alle in diesem Buch genannten Marken und Produktnamen unterliegen warenzeichen-, marken- oder patentrechtlichem Schutz bzw. sind Warenzeichen oder eingetragene Warenzeichen der jeweiligen Inhaber. Die Wiedergabe von Marken, Produktnamen, Gebrauchsnamen, Handelsnamen, Warenbezeichnungen u.s.w. in diesem Werk berechtigt auch ohne besondere Kennzeichnung nicht zu der Annahme, dass solche Namen im Sinne der Warenzeichen- und Markenschutzgesetzgebung als frei zu betrachten wären und daher von jedermann benutzt werden dürften.

Coverbild: www.purestockx.com

Verlag: VDM Verlag Dr. Müller Aktiengesellschaft & Co. KG
Dudweiler Landstr. 99, 66123 Saarbrücken, Deutschland
Telefon +49 681 9100-698, Telefax +49 681 9100-988, Email: info@vdm-verlag.de

Herstellung in Deutschland:
Schaltungsdienst Lange o.H.G., Berlin
Books on Demand GmbH, Norderstedt
Reha GmbH, Saarbrücken
Amazon Distribution GmbH, Leipzig
ISBN: 978-3-639-18206-4

Imprint (only for USA, GB)

Bibliographic information published by the Deutsche Nationalbibliothek: The Deutsche Nationalbibliothek lists this publication in the Deutsche Nationalbibliografie; detailed bibliographic data are available in the Internet at http://dnb.d-nb.de .

Any brand names and product names mentioned in this book are subject to trademark, brand or patent protection and are trademarks or registered trademarks of their respective holders. The use of brand names, product names, common names, trade names, product descriptions etc. even without a particular marking in this works is in no way to be construed to mean that such names may be regarded as unrestricted in respect of trademark and brand protection legislation and could thus be used by anyone.

Cover image: www.purestockx.com

Publisher:
VDM Verlag Dr. Müller Aktiengesellschaft & Co. KG
Dudweiler Landstr. 99, 66123 Saarbrücken, Germany
Phone +49 681 9100-698, Fax +49 681 9100-988, Email: info@vdm-publishing.com

Printed in the U.S.A.
Printed in the U.K. by (see last page)
ISBN: 978-3-639-18206-4

Khorshied Samad

Afghan Women, Media and Emerging Democracy

TABLE OF CONTENTS

ACKNOWLEDGMENTS

I would like to acknowledge the following people for their guidance and assistance in developing my book. Without their positive energies, feedback and gentle prodding, I would not have been able to complete this study, especially in such a concentrated period of time.

Professor Mark Lowes: thank you for your assistance, support and enthusiasm for my work and point of view. Your comments, suggestions and guidance were most helpful to me throughout this process. To all of the interview subjects who participated in this study: you contributed wonderful insight and rich perspective which made my work and experience so much more fulfilling.

Special thanks to my family and my husband's family for their love and encouragement. And, above all to my husband, Omar Samad, who has had great faith in my abilities despite my own trepidation, and has been a steadfast support throughout this process.

This work was originally completed as a Master's Thesis in July 2006, 2 weeks prior to the birth of our first son Soleiman, and defended at the University of Ottawa, Canada in November 2006. It is being published three years later in book form so there may be some discrepancies in reference to dates and passage of time.

This book is dedicated to my two boys, Soleiman and Arman, who bring sunshine and joy into my life each day. And, to the loving memory of my father, Hasan Nusratty, whose presence will help guide me for the rest of my days.

Khorshied Samad
July 2009
Paris, France

CHAPTER ONE:

INTRODUCTION: MEDIA AND DEMOCRACY

Myriad shapes of democracy have emerged throughout the years as political scientists have grappled with systems of liberal democracy, illiberal democracy, autocratic democracy and other derivatives, including deliberative democracy. Democracy as understood in the western discourse has its roots in the Greek city states, where it meant rule of the people (Zakaria, 2003). Western democracies are in the words of Aristotle "mixed regimes" (Aristotle, 1986). Huntington (1991b), however, writes in *The Third Wave,* "Elections, open, free and fair are the essence of democracy, the inescapable sine qua non" (p. 26).

In its functioning, democracy is a complex system that goes beyond the simple casting of ballots. Though society looks at voting as a minimal condition for democracy, an elective system of government is not necessarily a democratic system of government. Iceland established a democracy through a representative parliament in the tenth century, but it was not until the nineteenth century that English philosopher John Stuart Mill (1991) theoretically legitimated the concept of democracy as representative government. The debate among political theorists has been intense about the various forms of democracy.

An entirely new debate has arisen in the post-9/11 world we now live in as to whether democracy can and should take hold in countries of Eastern orientation and Middle Eastern origin. Specifically, in countries like Afghanistan, Iraq, and the Palestinian Territories, where democratic governments have been set up and "open, free and fair" elections have famously taken place, one has to wonder whether Western ideologies are an appropriate choice and can evolve with indigenous flavor in such ancient, windswept lands, laden with rich but strife-ridden histories.

This study aims to look at the fledging democracy now taking shape in Afghanistan, which only seven years ago was home to the most oppressive and cruel

Taliban regime, where human rights did not exist on any level, the press was completely state-controlled and male-dominated, and Afghan women were practically slaves in their own homes, unable to stroll freely, study or work in the light of day (Marsden, 1998). Theories of deliberative democracy will be explored against the evolving backdrop of Afghanistan, investigating the ideals set forth by scholarly sources in several key areas such the role of media, empowerment of women, and development of civil society in a post-conflict environment. The veracity of such ideals will be tested against the reality that now exists in this war-torn nation through a series of interviews of skilled experts on Afghanistan, and interpretive analysis of documentary sources and official reports from the United Nations, Afghan Government, and other world institutions and NGOs.

In his classic work from 1763, *The Social Contract,* Rousseau (1968) rejected representation as inconsistent with the idea of democracy, while political thinkers de Montesquieu (1914) and Locke (1970) - both supporters of separation of powers - adopted the concept that indirect democracy is necessary in growing societies. In more recent times, political scientist Dahl defined democracy as a "system of polyarchy". He outlined the fundamental pillars of polyarchy through seven attributes: (1) elected officials, (2) free and fair elections, (3) inclusive suffrage, (4) the right to run for office, (5) freedom of expression, (6) alternative information, and (7) associational autonomy (Dahl, 1971).

What distinguishes Western-style democracy from others throughout history is the evolving political tradition of "constitutional liberalism", which is defined by Zakaria as "the tradition that seeks to protect an individual's autonomy and dignity against coercion from state, church or society" (Zakaria, 2003, p.19). For the democracy optimists, the world has been shaped by the rise of democracy since the early 20th century and seen by a vast majority of people as, "the sole surviving source of political legitimacy" (Zakaria, 2003, p.13). Democracy optimists see the system as a way of life in the modern world transcending the fields of economics, culture, technology and even means of violence. In developed liberal societies with application of rule of law, separation of powers, freedom of expression, and protection of basic rights and property, the individual – and no longer the elites - is viewed as the economic agent, as well as the cultural icon and innovator of change.

Parekh (1993) disagrees with the optimist viewpoint. As he sees it the world is not made up of nations whose citizens consider the individual as the basic social unit because other systems, such as communal ones, also exist. He also espouses the view that "non-liberal" societies are not necessarily "illiberal." Democracy pessimists consider too much democracy as dangerous and a source of conflict, while others view shallow democracy as a cause of under-development or vice versa. Afghanistan is now seen to be a shallow democracy still very much in its infancy, with a great deal more time needed to develop its institutions, infrastructure, and to rebuild its socioeconomic foundations after nearly a quarter century of war. Inspired by Kant's *Perpetual Peace*[1] the political term "democratic peace" suggests that liberal democracies almost never go to war; whereas statistics show that there exists a strong record of conflict – interstate as well as civil – in non-democratic systems.

Huntington (1991a) identifies three historical or "long waves" of democracy. The first begins in the early 19th century until the 1920s. The reversal of the first wave begins with the accession of fascism in Italy in the early 1920s, followed by Hitler in Germany, and lasts until 1942, causing a reduction in the quantity of the world's democracies. The second wave begins with the end of World War II, pausing in 1962 till the mid-1970s with the rise of autocratic and militaristic regimes in Latin America, Africa and Asia. Since then democracy's third wave has added several dozen new democracies - notwithstanding Eastern Europe and East Asia - to its roster, and from all indications the wave has not yet crested. Benhabib (1996), a well-known deliberative democracy theorist, expands this concept by explaining that at least thirty more countries have attained democratic systems since 1993, adding to

---

[1] (Kant, 1947)

3

the twenty-one that had already reached that threshold by 1950. And, as stated previously, a new wave of democracy has been rising around the globe since the tragic events of 9/11.

One of the key pillars upholding democratic values and ideals in a democratic society is media. Media take on many roles, and flourish in an open, civil society. Media can point out injustices and imbalances in a democratic system, helping to keep it honest. Modern society tends to value media pluralism as an outcome over narrowed, subjective viewpoints. Democratic representation is preferred in our news and information which, theoretically, media provide. However, in today's polarized world, media can also reflect personal biases, governmental restrictions, and attempts at censorship, found in both Eastern and Western media worlds.

Notions of deliberative democracy take these ideas even further, focusing on how effective media are in fostering the notions of participation and active citizenship. Norris (2000) writes, "conceptions of representative democracy suggest three core roles for the news media: as a *civic forum* encouraging pluralistic debate about public affairs, as a *watchdog* guarding against the abuse of power, and as a *mobilizing* agent encouraging public learning and participation in the political process" (p. 7). The press, in this process, ensures the best possible participation of interested parties, helps people to choose between real alternatives by providing information to them, encourages debate on issues taken up by various parties and performs the 'watchdog' function of protecting against the tendency of the state to abuse the rights of its citizens. This can be especially important in post-conflict situations, where human rights and rule of law have yet to be established.

Barnett (2003) expounds upon this concept by underlining the importance of media in facilitating the development of democracy: "Media practices are particularly important here, in so far as modern print and broadcasting media have served as technologies for social integration over extended territorial scales, and have therefore been key to the institutionalization of democracy as expanded spatial

4

scales encompass large populations" (p. 74). Media are seen a critical factor in the "institutionalization of democracy", assisting in the articulation of social life and politics. In a post-conflict or developing nation, the ability of media to facilitate social integration and become a proponent of the development of civil society can become an influential factor.

Schudson (1995) writes that, "in a political democracy, the media are a vital force in keeping the concerns of the many in the field of vision of the governing few" (p. 20). In this manner, media's role is that of a balancing agent, guarding the polity from the narrow perspective and oppressive potential of the governing elite. Schudson goes on to elaborate that, "political reporting should keep citizens informed. Without accurate information about the views and values of candidates for office, a citizenry cannot cast intelligent ballots" (p. 26), and the populace cannot effectively monitor the government's operations and their chosen representatives' performances without adequate coverage in the media. This can be critical in a developing nation where infrastructures are lacking and a system of checks and balances is non-existent.

In post-conflict countries such as Afghanistan, where governments and democratic systems may be less developed and shallower, media usually struggle to establish a foothold. However, media's role in trying to foster the development of democracy in post-conflict situations is key, as expressed by Norris (2000) that, "this is especially important in newer democracies struggling to institutionalize a free press in the transition from authoritarian rule" (p. 12). Concepts such as freedom of the press or freedom of expression are foreign ideologies and lack historical reference in most non-western developing nations.

Media can serve as an empowering agent of democracy. In turn democracy nurtures and demands an effective system of media to facilitate in its own development. The two are intrinsically linked, aiding and supporting each other's growth: "Freedom of speech and association, as well as political equality, can clearly be justified simply as necessary for democracy" (Gould, 1996:179). Building on Dahl's work, Gutmann (1996) further elaborates on this in her discussion on 'polyarchies'. She states that 'polyarchies', or 'non-ideal democracies' outperform and justify themselves against undemocratic forms of government "by guarantees of free political speech, press, association, and equal suffrage for all adults, the right of all adults above a certain age to run for political office, the rule of law, and frequent, competitive elections that are procedurally fair" (pp. 340-1).

Today, media act as a cornerstone of democracy which impart information on public issues and through which citizens convey their opinions to policy-makers. In other words, media are the carrier of public opinion and play a crucial role in giving voice to people. Replacing the model of face-to-face communication or public gatherings of the past to discuss public issues, media today act as the mediator and facilitator between policy-makers and the citizenry. Various expectations from media include "reporting developments likely to impinge on the welfare of citizens; identifying key issues of the day and setting the political agenda; acting as spokesperson of various perspectives and interest groups; facilitating a dialogue between rulers and the public and across a diverse range of views" (Gurevitch & Blumler, 1995: 137).

Media have a significant role to play in every kind of society. There is no universal theory regarding the role of the press owing to different media systems in different settings. However, its role becomes crucial in a traditional and developing society – not only to monitor government actions or to provide information to citizens but also to highlight social and economic problems, and encourage progressive values to bring forth change. With the advent of media, Habermas' (1989) ideal of the public sphere has been broadened. Owing to the proliferation of modern technological societies, mass media have become imperative for the functioning of a democratic society. It is not an exaggeration to say that democracy and media are two sides of the same coin. In contemporary times no discussion on

6

the public sphere is complete unless it takes into account the role of media in representing concerns of citizens. They shape public consciousness, initiate debates, facilitate dialogue and are a major means of communication. Dahlgren (1991) regards media itself as the public sphere.

Bathla (1998) argues that media form a crucial part of the formal political sphere in a democratic society. However, after studying the role of women in media and how they are represented in media, she states that "one may legitimately question the democratic role of media in representing women's concerns and their participation in this public space" (p.16). Though women form half of the world's population she asserts that, "their concerns and status have remained marginal within the social, economic and political structures" (p. 16). This viewpoint could not be truer when one considers the current situation of Afghan women, who have had minimal representation in both the media and political sphere of their country until quite recently. The role of media in relation to women's empowerment is one area that has yet to be defined or truly investigated, and it is one that it difficult to measure by any standard. However, this work investigates some of these aspects in later chapters.

It was emphasized in this introduction that media help to uphold democratic principles as well as to shape democratic society. Media are today's opinion-makers and agenda-setters validating and legitimizing certain issues while rendering insignificance to others. The freedom granted to private media in a democratic society lies in the assumption that media service public interests. Therefore, it is crucial to understand the importance of media, the functions they are performing, and the responsibilities they are upholding or ignoring within a democratic society. The central research question guiding this study is what role media play in society or in the midst of social change.

The next chapter will investigate theories of deliberative democracy to better understand the requirements of media within democratic society. Various opinions and perspectives will be presented on media's role within society – both the positive and negative aspects – to gain a more complete grasp of the complex relationship that media and democracy share, especially in post-conflict and developing nations. The role of women in relation to media and democracy will also be discussed, insofar as how and in what manner gender is represented and supported by media in a democratic context.

CHAPTER TWO:

LITERATURE REVIEW

Using the current democratic and social transformation of Afghanistan as a backdrop, the discussion in this chapter examines how the seeds of deliberative democracy are being sown, and how the media are facilitating the development of emerging democracy and the political participation of Afghan women in Afghanistan today. Drawing on an analysis of scholarly literature, as well as a growing body of reports and studies from major international institutions, such as the United Nations, this chapter argues that theories of deliberative democracy help us to understand the role of media in post-conflict societies, shedding light on the importance of this element in developing civil society.

The Public Sphere

Deliberative democracy is most often associated with Habermas' (1989) notion of the public sphere, where he provides a model for the ideal performance of a democratic society and a guide for the ideal participation of media in that society. Later on in his work (1991), he defines the public sphere in terms of news media, conversation, and public opinion formation, stressing that media have become society's central means of disseminating information. He writes:

> By 'public sphere' we mean first of all a domain of our social life in which such a thing as public opinion can be formed. Access to the public sphere is open to all citizens. A portion of the public sphere is constituted in every conversation in which private persons come together to form a public. When the public is large, this kind of communication requires certain means of dissemination and influence; today, newspapers and periodicals, radio and television are the media of the public sphere (p. 398).

Habermas (1996) further refines his concept of the public sphere by stating that it can "best be described as a network for communicating information and points of view" (p. 389), where both negative and positive opinions have free room to be expressed and thereby contribute to a body of public opinion.

The public sphere concept has influenced an entire generation of deliberative democracy theorists. In some opinions, media are inseparable from the public sphere; they are often looked upon as one and the same. Numerous scholars have used the public sphere concept to analyze and evaluate the ways in which the organization of media, and broadcasting in particular, has served as a medium of political citizenship, for nurturing broader habits of sociability, and for expanding the scope of civic participation. For example, Schudson (1995) states that the notion of the public sphere directs attention to an analysis of media in terms of "the range of information the media make available to individual human minds, the range of connections they bring to light, the particular social practices and collective rituals by which they organize our days and ways" (p. 75).

Taking into consideration Habermas' notion of the public sphere, it follows that the key role of media is to provide information, giving equal weight to representation, while maintaining a separation from the influences of the state and market. Ideally then, media should seek to help redeem the promise of societal progress and participatory democracy by recognizing the voices of pluralism and diversity. Keane (1995) states that, "a fully democratic theory of public life would acknowledge the value of a diverse institutional infrastructure of mechanisms of accountability and representation to encourage pluralism and guard against the atrophied concentration of power" (p. 12). In open and egalitarian societies, pluralism and diversity are more often promoted within systems of government and media than in closed, non-democratic societies. It can be observed that in post-Taliban Afghanistan as emerging democracy strengthens so do the voices of pluralism and diversity.

Other deliberative democracy theorists expand upon this notion, most notably Sunstein, Goodin, and Thompson. According to Sunstein (2003), "the idea of a "public sphere", developed most prominently by Jurgen Habermas, can be understood as an effort to ensure a domain in which multiple views can be heard by people with multiple perspectives" (p. 95), supporting the necessity for pluralism and diversity. He adds that "it makes sense to promote ample social space both for enclave deliberation and for discussions involving a broad array of views, including those who have been within diverse enclaves" (p. 95). Here, Sunstein argues for a domain where multiple views – pluralist and diverse – can be heard in open deliberation along with full, uncensored information.

Goodin (2003) suggests that public opinion and multiple messages be presented through the filter of, "'mediated deliberation', where some intermediary filters what messages get passed along to others within the larger community…in modern mass society, much the same sort of 'mediated deliberation' occurs through the agency of the mass media" (p. 59). Goodin stresses the importance of limiting the flow of information to be filtered and edited through the mass media, controlling how much information anyone can impart to (or impose upon) everyone else. Perhaps too much information at once can be too overwhelming to absorb.

Thompson (1995) expands upon this train of thought, considering "media and communications as opening up spaces for *mediated deliberation*….in this way, modern media and communications technologies vastly expand the range of information, ideas and opinions made available to larger numbers of ordinary people than ever before" (p. 134). Thompson posits that one of the main contributions of modern communications technologies is in expanding the scope and power of public action, suggesting a stronger role for the mediated aspect of deliberative practice.

These deliberative democracy theorists argue that modern media create a domain where multiple views can be heard by the polity, allowing mediated deliberation, or discourses held within the media, to occur. This domain is

11

encapsulated most effectively in Habermas' (1989) notion of the public sphere, which is referred to in almost every subsequent deliberative democracy theory available today, and has become nearly synonymous with media itself.

Notions of Citizenship and Civic Participation

Barnett (2003) develops his argument about the significance of the public sphere in relation to civic participation, stating that "the public sphere concept has been used to develop understandings of media citizenship that focus upon the relationships between media and the practical capacities of participation in public life, broadly conceived" (p. 75). He defines media citizenship as, "overlapping rights to information, rights to receive and register opinions, and rights to fair and diverse representation" (p. 75). The concept of 'media citizenship' is exemplified in the West, where democratic tenets such as fair and equal representation in society, transparency, and access to information exist and are defended. These are not common aspects, or rights, which citizens of most Eastern, non-democratic societies have ready access to, however these same tenets have long been fought for the world wide over, especially in post-conflict or developing nations with a history of human rights abuses and dictatorial, oppressive governments such as Afghanistan (Goodson, 2001). Phillips (1996) explains that most citizens who suffer from 'economic inequality' or 'political exclusion' in an environment of 'systematic inequality' and shallow democracy never experience tenets which exist primarily in a 'robust democracy.' In her view, "robust democracy then becomes possible only when economic inequalities are substantially reduced" (p. 144), whereby economic opportunities help to sustain and fuel growth, peace and prosperity.

Cohen (1996) notes that the idea behind deliberative democracy is in insuring that all citizens have equal political rights, reducing inequalities of power, thereby reducing the incentive to "shift from deliberative politics to a politics of bargaining"

(p. 107). Furthermore, "many of the conventional, historical justifications for exclusions from or inequalities of political rights – justifications based on race and gender, for example – will not provide acceptable reasons in public deliberation" (p. 107). One could say that from Cohen's perspective, citizenship, as supported by deliberative democracy, demands a fair and just playing ground, free from prejudice or exclusionary practice. In Afghanistan's recent history, the opposite to Cohen's ideal of citizenship existed, however today there are inklings in the transformation of this nation which portend promising developments.

Gutmann (1996) argues that only deliberative democracy allows citizens to express their true natures through the process of deliberation, and that all other forms of government fall short. She states that, "the defense of democracy against traditional hierarchy, enlightened autocracy, liberal perfectionism, ultra-constitutionalism, and other credible political alternatives is weakened to the extent that we imagine a democracy that does not collectively deliberate over controversial matters of political importance" (p. 346). In her view, the power of deliberation cannot be underestimated in achieving fair and balanced civic participation by a politically active polity.

Based on the premise that any democracy is only as good as the participation of its citizens, theories of deliberative democracy posit that the formation of public opinion through engagement in discussions and debates about issues of the day lead to communicative action in the public sphere. Dryzek (2000) explains that, "communicative action is oriented to understanding between individuals rather than success in achieving predefined goals" (p. 22). This results in a greater quality of civil society, where political discussions and voting levels are higher, and the public's involvement is a critical factor in the development of a just and legitimate democracy. To this end, Dryzek states that "communicative rationality is found to the degree that communicative action is free from coercion, deception, self-deception, strategizing, and manipulation. Both forms of reason have their proper

13

place in human affairs" (p. 22). In this sense, the concept of communication free from coercion or manipulation is particularly relevant in developing or post-conflict countries where censorship and state-owned and controlled media are the norm. With a free media, the polity has a greater chance to express its views without fears of censorship or reprisal, and has greater access to information leading to higher levels of understanding and participation.

Moreover, the notion of citizenship demands that people make the time for participatory democracy. It is their civic responsibility, and duty, to contribute through healthy debate, in a type of public forum, to the formation of their society. According to Dahlgren (2000), "how we define citizenship is inseparable from how we define democracy and the good society" (p. 338). Consequently, an informed citizenry is essential to the functioning of democratic regimes. "The empirical evidence also demonstrates conclusively that knowledge is a critical element of democratic citizenship, as more informed citizens have civic attributes that characterize the qualities of good citizenship"(McGraw & Holbrook, 2003: 400). Better-informed citizens express more support for democratic norms and values such as tolerance and civil liberties, and are more likely to participate in politics through voting and elections. Schudson (2000) goes so far as to say that, "the news media *should* serve society by informing the general population in ways that arm them for vigilant citizenship" (p. 194).

In this manner, a public that is actively engaged in social discussion and politics through rational-critical discourse contributes to the legitimacy of modern democracy. In the words of Calhoun (1992) "a public sphere adequate to a democratic polity depends upon both quality of discourse and quantity of participation" (p. 2). Similarly, Cunningham (2002) supports the notion that a "democracy is at its most robust when there is energetic citizen participation in taking collective action, in its ideal form in local forums like town hall meetings or voluntary associations" (p. 24).

These viewpoints on active citizen participation through discussions in open forums are translated into reality in Afghanistan, where a long held, respected tradition of the *Loya Jirga* (Grand Assembly) and *Shuras* (Gathering of Tribal Elders) has existed for hundreds of years, and is still used today for purposes of deliberation about important issues of community and national importance (Rawan, 2002). According to Benhabib (1996), "it is central to the model of deliberative democracy that it privileges such a public sphere of mutually interlocking and overlapping networks and associations of deliberation, contestation, and argumentation" (p. 74), stressing the significance of deliberative bodies in such a public sphere, the rationale for parliamentary opposition, the need for a "free and independent media", and the importance of "employing majority rule as a decision procedure" (p. 84).

An *Emergency Loya Jirga* was held in Kabul in June 2002, to vote for the Transitional Government of Afghanistan, placing Hamid Karzai in the position of Transitional President. A *Constitutional Loya Jirga* was held in December 2003, ratifying the new Constitution of Afghanistan in January 2004, and setting the political stage for the first Presidential Democratic Elections, held in October 2004, and Parliamentary Elections, held in September 2005 (The Europa World Book, 2005).

Due to United Nations insistence following the Bonn Agreement of December 2001, which stipulated that a gender-sensitive government be formed following the defeat of the Taliban regime, Afghan women participated in both of these historic *Loya Jirga* gatherings (Abirafeh, 2005). They were nominated as political representatives of their provinces, and there was even one woman, Dr. Masouda Jalal, who ran as the first female candidate ever in the Presidential Democratic Elections in October 2004.

However, Afghan women representation is solely lacking in the *Shuras*, where tribal elders and village leaders discuss and deliberate about important community

15

matters which affect the entire village. Afghan women are denied access and participation in these gatherings (Nawabi, 2003).

Therefore, though aspects of deliberative democracy exist in the traditions of the *Loya Jirga* and the *Shuras*, Afghan women are not normally included in these important forums of discussion and deliberation. Their voices are silenced and marginalized as they are throughout most aspects of Afghan society (United Nations Development Programme (UNDP), 2002). This reality is in stark contrast to what Mansbridge (1999) states when she says that, "in a good democracy, large or small, the deliberative arena should ideally be equally open to all, and power – in the sense of the threat to sanction or the use of force – should not interfere with the impact of the better argument" (p. 48).

According to the importance attributed to deliberation within the framework of an active polity, it is through the lens of public attention to critical issues and discourse that public opinion is filtered to its most truthful core. In most democratic societies, it is media that provides the platform for expression and dissemination of public opinion and information to the citizenry. Barber (1998) adds further to this viewpoint by stating that, "democratic theory has traditionally interpreted the media as crucial to a civil society, since they afford us free communication and diversified information" (p. 51). However seen as crucial to the development of democracy and civil society, Barnett (2003) argues that "media and communications are neither obstacles to genuine participation and authentic representation, nor the potential solution that can reconnect rulers and ruled in harmonious union" (p. 3).

There has to be another basis for unity within a communicative polity, another reason for healthy social cohesion. The complex role of media in society with its inherent ability to foster democratic as well as undemocratic principles is not easily explained or identified, just as democracy is notoriously difficult to define.

Role of the Media

According to Dahlgren (2001), "the media have become the major sites, the privileged space of politics in late modern society. Here we have the key to understanding the media's role in reshaping democracy" (p. 84). He further expands upon this idea by stating that media are without a doubt incredibly important in helping make politics and society visible, in providing information, analysis, and a public sphere where civic culture can be shared. This role appears to be continually expanding in the modern era. Additionally, Dahlgren asserts that the media have been "instrumental in globalizing the normative vision of democracy," and are "an integral part of our contemporary reality, a major historical force" (p. 64). Media have helped spread the values and tenets of Western democracy throughout the modern world, pushing various messages out across the globe.

Dahlgren clearly underscores the media's key role in the transformation of democracy, especially in Western democratic societies, and illustrates that media can be an important resource for participation in both the politics and culture of society. Thompson (1995) further elaborates upon the media's role when he states that, "at the macro, societal and micro level of everyday life, the modern world – and democracy in particular – would be totally unrecognizable without the media of communication" (p. 135), so crucial is media's role in the formation of modern-day democratic society.

In a country like Afghanistan where democracy is fragile and in an early state of development, there are many powers at play tugging at the fabric of this process. Many actors appear to be intent on disrupting the spread of democracy and the fledgling Afghan government. (Integrated Regional Information Networks (IRIN), 2006). Young (2003) posits that "practices of deliberative democracy also aim to bracket the influence of power differentials in political outcomes, because agreement between deliberators should be reached on the basis of argument, rather than as a

17

result of threat or force" (p. 103). This assumes that deliberation can and will take place between political factions, citizens and the government. The Afghan parliament, newly inducted on December 19th, 2005, provides a forum where such deliberation should take place if open discussion and dialogue is encouraged and not suppressed or censored.

However, Young (1996) also states that, "parliamentary debates or arguments in court are not simply free and open public forums in which all people actually have the right to express claims and give reasons according to their own understanding...deliberation is competition" (p. 123). Often, in these same environments, norms of deliberation are 'culturally specific' and "often operate as forms of power that silence or devalue the speech of some people" (Young, 1996: 123). More often than not, the voices of women and minorities are the ones that are silenced or marginalized, especially in forums such as parliament or Loya Jirgas, where men, not women, historically are given free reign to express themselves.

Where media are state-owned and controlled, content is usually censored and information filtered by the governing elite; this occurs even outside of state controlled media. For democracy to flourish information needs to be free and diverse, reflecting the voices of pluralism. Against this background, Schudson (2000) explains, the role of public and privately owned media in more liberal, open societies as being a state of affairs where "state-operated media in authoritarian political systems serve directly as agents of state social control, both public and privately owned media in liberal societies carry out a wider variety of roles, cheerleading the established order, alarming the citizenry about flaws in that order, providing a civic forum for political debate, acting as a battleground among contesting elites" (p.181). Media in this regard fulfill a highly complex role in open, democratic societies, taking on "watchdog" characteristics as well as ideally providing a platform for inherent aspects of the political process to be discussed and analyzed.

18

This is why access to information is so important for the citizenry to become politically active agents in the development and management of their society. Access to information is a powerful, mobilizing force, and mass media generally are the providers of this information. "Information allows people to make good choices. People who do not have access to information are discriminated in a way similar to those denied the vote a century ago. Without information, people choose irrationally" (Calsamiglia, 1999: 138). It can be argued that people also choose irrationally even when they have access and information.

The same holds true for the importance of education. Without access to education or literacy, a citizenry cannot understand or absorb information necessary to become an active polity. They will not be able to comprehend the printed word in the press or the Internet, or to understand the depth of issues being deliberated in most media. Dahlgren (2000) stresses that education is crucial for a healthy democracy because literacy is essential for democratic citizenry. Developing this point further, he argues that people must also have the ability to express their own ideas if they are to partake in the public spheres' processes of opinion formation and/or engage in other political activities. To this end he emphasizes that, "communicative competencies are indispensable for a democratic citizenry" (p.123). This is why radio is still the most dominant form of media in Afghanistan, where nearly 70 percent of the population is illiterate, with those levels reaching close to 96 percent for Afghan women in the rural areas (Kandiyoti, 2005; Rawan, 2002). Radio is a cheap and efficient form of media, transcending problems of illiteracy and lack of power. Radio is mobile and fluid, easily traveling into the far corners of remote Afghanistan. And, radio can be a private and powerful medium carrying crucial information to thousands of listeners, or educational messages to a select few.

Regardless of the media's benefits to society and the formation of democracy, the belief that the media are biased is pervasive. This charge is for the most part focused on the press, as the broadcast media historically have been subject to greater

19

regulation that constrains impartial news coverage. However, as mentioned previously, in our post-9/11 world even these regulations have been stretched and affected by biases and fears. According to McGraw (2003), "the existence of media bias has enormous implications for the quality of democracy, because citizens would be receiving distorted information that would undermine their ability to act in their self-interest or in the collective good" (p. 404). Elaborating on this claim, McGraw notes that the empirical evidence from studies of the mainstream press in North America points to "patterns of neutrality rather than bias, with no systematic tendency to favor one side of the ideological spectrum over the other" (p. 405). Therefore there is no definitive agreement reached by scholars in this arena of discussion on media bias.

A similar type of argument arises with the discussion of the news media's increasingly more negative and cynical coverage of politics. It has been argued by many theorists such as Putnam (2000) and Katz (1998) that the media's negativism is responsible for political cynicism in the public, as well as declining civic engagement, knowledge, and participation. This perspective has come to be known as the media (or video) malaise theory (Thompson, 1978), giving rise to one of the most dynamic debates about the role of mass media and democracy in modern societies. There is little doubt that media coverage (especially of U.S. politics) has become more negative and critical, smacking of 'yellow journalism' and mud-slinging tendencies from the early 19th century press (Schudson, 1992), and continues to sensationalize and exploit negative aspects of the news.

Expounding upon these negative traits found within the media, Barnett (2003) explains that, "a number of commentators identify the media as bearing primary responsibility for the decline of active citizenship and the decay of democratic institutions" (p. 3). The media are charged with "encouraging cognitive dependence, narcosis and the attenuation of critical faculties"; "eroding the capacity of citizens to trust in public institutions and hold them accountable"; "undermining the autonomy of science and a robust public culture of criticism"; and, with "encouraging widespread civic disengagement and the withering of social capital" (Barnett, 2003: 3). These are hefty charges made against the media, which are as vilified here as they are praised and adorned in just as many other scholarly circles[2].

Putnam (2000) posits that there is overwhelming evidence linking television watching (more specifically watching entertainment vs. news) and civic disengagement in American society. However, he goes on to say that, "television at its civic best can be a gathering place, a powerful force for bridging social differences, nurturing solidarity, and communicating essential civic information" (p. 243). Similarly, Katz (1998) argues that, "in fact, television both contributes and discontributes to democracy" (p. 94). He goes on to elaborate, "that the technology of radio ultimately weakened the parliament while favoring the national leaders, that television weakened the political party system and grass-roots participation, and that new media – cable, satellite, and computer-mediation – are presently undermining the solidarity of the nation from both within and without" (p. 98). Here, both the positive and negative aspects of media, and more specifically television, are exemplified.

Norris (2000) expresses a more encouraging viewpoint about the relationship between media and political participation, stating that:

> Contrary to the videomalaise hypothesis, use of the news media is positively associated with a wide range of indicators of political knowledge, trust and mobilization. People who watch more TV news, read more newspapers, surf the net, and pay attention to campaigns, are consistently more knowledgeable, trusting of government, and participatory (p. 10).

---

[2] See, for example, Norris (2000) and Dahlgren (1991).

In other words, according to Norris, the relationship between news exposure and civic attitudes and behavior is the reverse of that predicted by the media malaise hypothesis.

Barnett (2003, p. 33) best sums up how media often get the brunt of criticisms and accusations from scholars and political theorists bent on holding media responsible for massive shifts in modern-day life, as well as a decline in civic participation. He writes:

> Modern political theory connects the legitimacy of democratic rule to the capacities of citizens to exercise reasonable political judgment through the medium of public communication" and oftentimes the "acceleration of processes of media communication and information transfer undermines the norms of reasoned debate and discussion upon which democratic participation depends.

Again, there does not appear to be a definitive agreement among scholars and political theorists regarding the complex role of media within society, or its impact on the development of democracy. It is difficult to prove or measure the positive and negative impact or influence that media have in modern-day society.

The democratic potential of all forms of media is far-reaching and broad. Not only does it disperse essential information through multiple sites or spheres, it also renders public life accessible to all through various means, as well as encourages the consideration of multiple voices and perspectives. According to Lacey (1996), from this perspective it becomes possible to recognize that "the development of mass communication and broadcasting, in particular, rather than being a nail in the coffin of the public sphere, represented its extension and reinvigoration" (p. 235). In this light, media encourage discourse and discussions about important issues of the day, providing critical information to the public.

Media practices are particularly important here, especially with regard to modern print and broadcasting media as they have served as far-reaching technologies for social integration. Therefore, they have been "key to the institutionalization of democracy as expanded spatial scales encompassing large populations. But more than simply stretching social life and politics, different media practices articulate and rearticulate different socio-spatial scales: the nation-state and the home, everyday life and formal public realms" (Barnett, 2003, p. 7). Moreover, the media create a platform in today's world where various interests can potentially be brought together, "permitting a rational, well-informed conversation between equals capable of resolving their differences by non-coercive means" (Schlesinger & Tumber, 1995: 9). This is the goal of communication in an open, democratic society.

Both democracy and media thus form a part of the public sphere and enjoy a very close relationship. In other words, a democratic society cannot function without a free media representing public interests, and the media thrive in a robust democracy where multiple views can be shared and openly discussed. The role of media is critical to a healthy democracy where citizens can fairly and equally participate in society.

Civil Society, Freedom of the Press, and Human Rights

The democratic tradition and freedom of the press go hand-in-hand. Most constitutions worldwide, especially in democratic societies, enshrine the principles of freedom of speech, freedom of expression, and freedom of the press. "The doctrine of freedom of speech took birth in liberal political philosophy whereby it was recognized that freedom of speech, especially in the form of freedom of the press, had an important political role to play in a democracy" (Bathla, 1998, p. 14). Even in the Afghan Constitution of 1964, these principles were upheld and protected, only to be revoked and reinstalled with the passing of subsequent political regimes (World Press Encyclopedia, 2003).

Increasingly, there has been an attempt by some commentators to create a view of 'civil society' where the media hold a vital role, not only in dispersing free and accessible information essential for the active citizenry, but also in helping to uphold the most meaningful tenants of democracy and principles of free expression. Taras (2001) states that, "simply put, the communications system is the spinal cord of national existence and of a democratic society. If it is severed or disrupted in some way, then a country risks losing touch with its sensory system and citizens risk being disconnected from each other" (p. 115). In a country like Afghanistan, oftentimes it is only through media such as radio or print that outlying rural areas have any connection to the cities or matters of national importance, let alone international news (Razi, 1994).

Cohen (1996) asserts that any form of democracy or intelligent decision-making needs to recognize deliberation and discussion as critical, especially for the protection of rights within society. To this end, he writes that "the deliberative view will provide a basis for wider guarantees of basic liberties", extending naturally from religious liberty to "a wide guarantee of expressive liberty" (p. 102). The practice of deliberative democracy, he argues, would create a citizenry more educated and engaged in the politics of governance, and "would thus lead to a stronger and more stable society that would better protect human rights" (p. 102). In his view, deliberative democracy would, therefore, contribute to the creation of a more just and communication-driven society.

The fact that there are people within society without a voice, or denied equal representation, affects the legitimacy of democracy. According to Calsamiglia (1999), the best form of democracy treats all citizens with equal concern, producing substantial results affecting the entire polity. He argues that "without universal

24

consideration and respect for new participants, there is no legitimacy" (p. 141). This parallels the views of Manin (1997) who posits that, principles of free expression are critical in effective systems of media and communication because they underpin diversity and pluralism, while simultaneously ensuring legitimacy through civic participation within a democracy.

In terms of fledgling democracies, or "highly unequal societies" such as Afghanistan, Barnett (2003) states that "media exposure remains a crucial resource for pressuring powerful institutions to act in accord with publicly accepted norms rather than from narrow private interest" (p. 65). He goes on to point out that public exposure of injustices can serve to break the cycle by which "social and economic inequality reinforces political inequality" (p. 65). Effectively used, channels of media communication can promote a 'politics of shame', whereby societal issues and promises can be monitored and held accountable in the public eye. In helping to uphold freedom of expression and rights of participation media institutions are "therefore crucial to the instrumental realization of normative principles of democracy, equality and social justice" (Sen, 1999: 23).

Barber (1998) asserts that "civil society is not an alternative to democratic government but, rather, the free space in which democratic attitudes are cultivated and democratic behavior is conditioned" (p. 6). In a country such as Afghanistan where more than 23 years of war and social upheaval have damaged the infrastructure within every sector of society and have traumatized the psyche of the Afghan people, democratic attitudes and behavior may take a long time to develop (Abirafeh, 2005). These are not cultural traits that come naturally to a people; however, they can be taught and learned through education, examples of other Muslim democracies, and exposure in the media.

Media play a key role in educating and empowering a public, especially in the knowledge and establishment of their human rights. Sassi (2001) states that "while the precise meaning of civil society is far from settled, it is now generally agreed that

25

the mass media have an extraordinary impact on its forms and functions." (p. 93). She offers a further explanation of civil society as "the sphere where common concerns can be identified and made political. Today many scholars and activists see a strong civil society as a crucial component of an inclusive and democratic society" (pg. 106). In Afghanistan, both civil society and democracy are in the infancy of their development. Clearly, as democratic renewal is tied to civic renewal, these social processes will take time to take hold, and there may be many steps backwards before real progress has been made. Western sensibilities that are attune to rapid change will have to refocus their energies and expectations with a large dose of patience and a different mindset.

Empowerment of Women

The issue of gender is a timely and hotly contested subject in Afghanistan, as it still is, or has been, in the recent past of most countries. To the extent that media represent and support women in a modern-day context is an area of critical importance to this study. Whether media help to provide a voice for women, and specifically in this case Afghan women, is a key point of discussion in this work. According to Landes (1996), "from the outset, democracy in the modern world produced not only a discourse but a practice of gender difference" (p. 296), contributing to the imbalance and inequality of women in most societies.

Feminist theorists staunchly condemn patterns of social development which reveal measures of inequality and repression against women and minorities. Feminist political theory argues that democratic political foundations have been gender-biased and suffer from various discrepancies that prevent the participation of women in the political/public sphere and limit their role as political citizens. Within forums of collective deliberation, legitimacy is defined by the free and equal participation of its citizens. Benhabib (1996) argues that collective decision-making processes reflect the highest levels of legitimacy and rationality, "only if such decisions are in principle open to appropriate public processes of deliberation by free and equal citizens" (p. 69).

However, Landes notes that "the democratic public sphere appears to be essentially and not just accidentally "masculinist" (p. 82). Similarly Young (1996) expresses concern that since most political theory demands the need for homogeneity, women and radicalized groups, or minorities, find themselves automatically excluded. In the words of Gould (1996), "this universal sphere, even within the confines of a nation or a political unit, is less than universal in its constitution" (p. 175). What is written in the laws of the land is rarely reflected in the reality of everyday life.

Cohen (1996) argues that "as innumerable feminists have insisted, the public/private dichotomy has thereby served to reinforce and perpetuate social hierarchies and inequity between the sexes in all spheres of life" (p. 189). This has denied women full membership in the political community and equal opportunity in economic life. Thus, women's civic participation and citizenship have been severely curtailed by "legal, practical and discursive barriers" that were erected against their becoming full citizens, and from participating in the public domain at all (J. L. Cohen, 1996: 189). In Cunningham's (2002) view, "discrimination in everyday life perpetuates political discrimination now masquerading as universally accessible democracy" (p. 21). In other words, the inequities and prejudices run deep under the surface appearance of equality and democracy for all. Democracy does not necessarily provide "life, liberty and the pursuit of happiness" for all.

Deliberative democrats, however, are also known for support of social activism of the women's and other social movements. For example, Benhabib (1996), Gutmann and Thompson (1996) view deliberative democracy as being mainly designed to justify anti-oppressive values and policies. Hence, Cohen (1996) insists that "conventional, historical justifications for exclusion from or inequalities

27

of political rights based on such things as race or gender are incompatible with public deliberation" (p. 180). Indeed, essential characteristics of the public sphere as a concept are that it allows free and equal participation in public debate and that debate is free of domination (Fraser, 1992).

According to Bathla (1998), "a certain universalism regarding the subordinate status of women exists in most human societies. History might vary in terms of time, space, and actors, but the issue of women's oppression or women struggling to enter the political sphere share a commonality giving rise to global feminism or the notion of sisterhood" (p. 36). In most national histories, countries have idealized the private virtues of women and public roles of men. With the exception of Scandinavian countries, women's participation in national and local politics has remained incredibly low. Most of the public places like government institutions, courts, police, workplaces, etc., according to Pateman (1988), look like men's clubs "from all of which women are excluded or to which they are mere auxiliaries" (p.210). Democracy has not recognized women as political citizens in the fullest sense, due to which women's participation in public life has remained low.

On the other hand, media have often been viewed as champions for women's rights and supporters of their civic participation in society. From the early days of the print media, women wrote about their condition not simply to 'voice' their concerns but even more to transform, or at least to affect, the social traditions pertaining to gender relations. Women's entry into the public life of formal politics in early twentieth-century Europe and North America coincided with the development of broadcasting, which was understood as an inherently public medium (Sakr, 2004b).

"Historically, the rise of concerns over massification, in politics, society and culture, was related to the political and economic enfranchisement of women, leading to the paradigmatic form of analysis that saw the decline of serious public culture as following on from a feminization of the public sphere. The meanings of

28

masculinity, femininity, public and private, and media are indissolubly connected to each other" (Lacey, 1996: 110) However, women's position within media power structures and media representation of women are persistent concerns in every society, because negative stereotyping and lack of female input reflect and reinforce wide gender inequalities.

A big part of empowering women lies in ensuring that they have the means through the mass media to express their own opinions about inequalities on their own behalf. In the very act of obligating states to eliminate 'all forms' of discrimination against women, the Convention on the Elimination of All Forms of Discrimination Against Women (CEDAW) requires signatory states to find out what women themselves think about laws, policies and practices (Kandiyoti, 2005; Nawabi, 2003). Afghanistan is one of many signatory states with CEDAW. Due to the low civic participation of Afghan women and ongoing cultural restrictions against their involvement in public life it is very difficult to ascertain an accurate reflection of their viewpoints about the inequalities they face. However, Afghan media and, in particular, Afghan women journalists, are beginning to break these cultural barriers within the development of a dynamic new media movement in Afghanistan (Kandiyoti, 2005).

Since the fall of the Taliban in late 2001, there has been a steady increase of local and international coverage about Afghan women's issues, helping to expose the many challenges and inequities they struggle against. This coverage also underlines the need for better understanding of the influences at play in regions where women-media interaction has not been researched (The World Bank, 2005). Media industries play a pivotal role in organizing the images and discourse through which people make sense of the world. According to Sakr (2004a) "in today's changing media landscape in the Middle East and North Africa, questions arise as to whether the changes are empowering women" (p. 2).

29

The Middle East media have changed dramatically since the early 1990s and women's voices have grown in audibility over the same period. "Yet it is rare to see the altered landscape for public communication analyzed in terms of how it relates to the changing climate for empowerment of women" (Sakr, 2004b). It is very difficult to measure levels of empowerment of women in any sense, let alone through the media. However, one of the clearest messages to be derived from various studies such as the Global Media Monitoring Project and attempts at analyzing women's empowerment in the media has been that most voices are stifled, especially in non-western societies, and that women's voices are stifled worst of all.

Some argue that media are a male establishment and news is a man's world, i.e., it is about men, by men, and overwhelmingly seen through men. According to Bathla (1998),

> The silence of the media on women's issues and the movement also hints at the insignificance attached to women as citizens and to their participation in the public sphere. In other words, media has rendered insignificance to women's voices and conveyed that their concerns are irrelevant to democratic polity thus also indicating that a free press in itself cannot guarantee representation of opinions and values of marginalized sections (p. 109).

In discriminating between male and female voices, neither Afghanistan nor the Middles East as a whole is alone. Wider margins for freedom of expression in other parts of the world are not necessarily matched by equal opportunities for women in media industries or by media coverage that adequately represents women. A study of US film and prime-time television in the mid- to late 1990s described women's employment history and outlook as 'dismal', and a 2006 report shows surprisingly that fewer women are being represented in key media roles than ever before (Rivers, 2006).

Perhaps it is not women who change the news, but changes within the news that open the way for women to participate. According to Sakr (2004), "If gender boundaries are negotiated through the media, it is also because the media provide an interface between the private and public spheres, through which the categories of public and private can be contested" (p. 13). Media may or may not be facilitators of women's empowerment; however media have provided channels of communication whereby women have been able to 'voice' their concerns and needs to a public that previously had neither exposure nor access to these hidden matters. It is in this manner that media are such a powerful force, bringing a myriad of heretofore unheard voices and concerns into the world spotlight. Media continue to help provide women with a much needed platform of expression in an unequal social landscape.

Central Research Question

In the light of developments outlined above, the central research question guiding the book is: "*what role do the media play in the midst of or in relationship to social change?*" In order to address this question, the work investigates the key themes drawn from the scholarly literature of the previous sections of this chapter, exploring these areas within the framework of the primary source interviews and findings, and, finally, expanding upon the role that media play in promoting the development of democracy and civil society in post-conflict nations such as Afghanistan.

The next chapter presents a brief history of Afghanistan, focusing on recent political developments, media development, Afghan women's issues and challenges, and their potential role in the reconstruction of their country. It will be argued that media in the past, as well as currently, have played a crucial role in the development of democracy in this war-torn nation. It will also be shown that Afghan women have been given a significant opportunity to contribute to the social reawakening of their country, despite the overwhelming obstacles they continue to face on a daily basis.

CHAPTER THREE:

AFGHANISTAN: A BRIEF HISTORY

The current situation in Afghanistan provides an interesting test bed for examining the role of media and ideals of deliberative democracy in developing and/or post-conflict societies. The discussion in this chapter will examine the extent to which the media facilitates the development of emerging democracy and the social and political participation of Afghan women in Afghanistan by looking at recent political history, attempts at reform, and media development in this war-torn nation.

From Conflict to Post-Conflict

Afghanistan is a devastated country emerging from the depths of 23 years of war, geopolitical and social upheaval. It is one of the most impoverished countries on earth, with some of the highest levels of maternal and infant mortality, illiteracy and post-conflict struggle (United Nations Development Programme (UNDP), 2002). Every sector in society has been damaged or destroyed, and now the Afghan people are engaged in a process of rebuilding their country with the assistance of the international donor community.

Afghanistan's democratization and rebuilding efforts over the past four years cannot be well understood without a quick review of the country's modern-day political history and socio-economic dynamics. The country's internal political development, its foreign relations, and its existence as an independent state have been largely determined by its location. Waves of migration in ancient times left a human residue to form a mosaic of ethnic and linguistic groups. Invading armies and dynasties as far West as Greece and as far East as Mongolia passed through the region establishing, at least temporary, local control and often dominating Persia and northern India as well.

Afghanistan did not become a truly independent nation until the twentieth century, and for centuries remained a zone of conflict among strong neighboring powers. The area's heterogeneous groups were not bound into a single political entity until 1747, when the first Afghan dynasty was established and ruled the country until 1973. Just as it was the arena of conflict between the Mughol Empire of India and the Safavi Empire of Persia between the 16th and 18th centuries, Afghanistan in the 19th and early 20th centuries lay as a buffer state between the expanding might of the Russian and British empires (The Europa World Book, 2005). (Also, see Appendix I).

The country gained full independence in 1919. Thereafter, it followed a policy of neutrality followed by non-alignment with growing economic and military ties to the Soviet Union, as a result of a tilt by the West toward Pakistan and Iran. As a poor landlocked agricultural and nomadic country with few untapped resources but strong potential for trade and transit, it reached self-sufficiency in foodstuff but solicited foreign aid or capital to build modern infrastructures. During the Cold War, the rulers took advantage of East-West rivalries to engage in some development, institution-building and modernization. These changes led to a period of liberalization in the 1960s and 70s, ending a 10-year long flirtation with a constitutional monarchy and a freely elected parliament in 1973 (Dupree, 1977). However, due to weak commitment by the monarch to build a democratic foundation and allow formal political party activity, the monarchy was overthrown. By 1978 the country drifted toward a takeover by pro-Moscow Marxist-Leninist parties that had established strong influence in the Soviet-trained army (The World Fact Book, 2005).

The Soviet Union, fearing a setback caused by popular rebellion, invaded the Central Asian nation in 1979. Afghanistan became the last battleground of the Cold

War as the US and others covertly supported anti-Soviet forces, mainly through neighboring Pakistan. Thousands of Muslims from other countries poured into Afghanistan to take part in the "Jihad." More than 5 million Afghans fled to neighboring countries. By 1989 the USSR withdrew and by 1992 the victorious Islamic factions were themselves embroiled in a new round of power struggles fuelled by most of Afghanistan's neighbors. In contrast, the West disengaged and did not attempt to encourage a political solution or make any significant efforts at post-conflict rebuilding (Anwar, 1988; Hyman, 1992).

Meanwhile, a new militia named the Taliban emerged in 1994 and took control of Kabul in 1996 (Marsden, 1998). Backed by radical elements in Pakistan and other countries from the Gulf region, they were originally viewed by some western nations, including the US, as a stabilizing force. In reality, the Taliban, who were mostly students from radical madrassas (religious schools), operated outside a constitutional framework. Their justice was based on a narrow understanding of Islamic and Sharia law. They lacked legitimacy and relied heavily on support from radical networks that advocated hard-line Islamic ideology. Human rights abuses, particularly of ethnic and religious minorities and disenfranchisement of women, were widespread (Rashid, 2000). Under the Taliban's draconian regime, Afghanistan became a haven for terrorist groups, in particular al-Qaeda, and a major producer of opiates (Rashid, 2000). US-led military action coupled with Afghan militia attacks in response to al-Qaeda's terrorist attacks of September 11th, 2001, led to the overthrow of the Taliban regime.

As Parekh observed, "how a polity combines liberalism and democracy or how liberal and democratic it chooses to be depends on its history, traditions, values, problems and needs" (1993, p. 160). This necessitates that they work out their own political destiny according to their particular historical and political background. That is why a roadmap was negotiated in December 2001, at the UN-sponsored Bonn Conference on the future of Afghanistan, where anti-Taliban and other factions were included and agreed to a transitional process leading to elections for a "broad-based, gender-sensitive, multi-ethnic and fully representative government" (UNAMA, 2001, p. 5).

The Afghan Interim Authority under the leadership of Hamid Karzai was established for a six-month period. An Emergency Loya Jirga (traditional grand council), met in June 2002 and elected Karzai as the Chairman of the Afghan Transitional Authority, which governed the country until a constitution was ratified and elections were held. Following heated debates, the new Afghan Constitution was adopted by a Constitutional Loya Jirga in January 2004 (Government of Afghanistan, 2004).

Nationwide presidential elections were held under international supervision in October 2004. Despite some complications, the presidential election process, including unfettered campaigning and media access, was widely assessed as being a success by the international community. Hamid Karzai won garnering 55 percent of the vote. Despite border infiltrations and threats from Taliban insurgents, the turnout was 8.1 million or 70 percent of registered voters, 40 percent of whom were women. Karzai was sworn in as Afghanistan's first democratically elected President in December 2004 (The World Fact Book, 2005).

Completing the provisions of the Bonn Agreement, on September 18th, 2005, more than 5800 candidates, including former reformed Taliban and communists, took part in elections for the lower house of parliament (*Wolesi Jirga*) and for 34 provincial councils based on the seldom used single, non-transferable voting system. This meant that candidates did not run on party rosters. The results announced in early November showed a rainbow Parliament, with 26 percent of the 249 seats going to women in the lower house (Nawabi, 2003).

State and Nation-Building

As a result of war and destruction, Afghanistan experienced severe migration, a brain drain, collapse of its civil and military institutions, erosion of infrastructure, accumulation of weapons and criminalization of the economy. The education and health systems came to a grinding halt and large swaths of the country were turned into minefields, endangering farming and herding. The influence of extremist and radical Islam reached its peak under the Taliban. Human rights and gender equality suffered as a fledgling civil society collapsed under the weight of conflict. Following the retreat of the Soviet Army, Afghan factions, increasingly organized along ethnic lines and to varying degrees beholden to more powerful regional powers, could not agree on a national political settlement. In the absence of international engagement, the country fell off the radar screen. Meanwhile, international terrorist cells found an unruly fertile ground for setting up their headquarters and training camps. The impoverished nation joined the rank of failed states, which added to the legacy of tragedy gripping this war-ravaged country (Goodson, 2001).

Following the attacks of September 11th, 2001, a US-led offensive helped Afghans bring down the Taliban. Furthermore, the political synergy created by the Afghan willingness to give peace a chance, backed by the international community's re-engagement to help in state and nation-building was the catalyst for real change. The process was backed by two major financial and technical commitments pledged at the 2002 Tokyo and 2004 Berlin Conferences for reconstruction. The donor countries promised to commit more that $13 billion in aid for the period 2002 to 2008. To date, the disbursements, partly managed by the World Bank and other world institutions, amount to approximately $ 4 billion, only a quarter of which has gone directly to the Afghan government (The World Bank, 2004). The US contribution thus far amounts to almost 50 percent of the whole.[3]   There   are

---

[3] These figures do not include expenditures toward military operations.

signs of growing disenchantment with the way reconstruction has been executed, as illustrated by the recent election of populist and anti-corruption candidates to parliament (Coleman & Hunt, 2006). The Afghan people have been made many promises and expected to see more tangible change in their everyday lives five years after the fall of the Taliban. However, after nearly a quarter century of war and destruction, perhaps everyone's expectations for change are unrealistically high.

Liberal Foundations and Civil Society

Following the second "liberation" in 2001, Afghanistan seemed to have no option but to take the "weak-state path" (Tilly, 2002: 196) to start the process of democratization. However, the Bonn Accord prescribed a fast-track path. Today, women, free media, NGOs and the private sector constitute the four pillars of a blossoming civil society that is challenging centuries-old traditions and mentalities. According to Parekh, in a democracy, civil society "is the realm of interest and choice *par excellence*. It stands for the totality of relationships voluntarily entered into by self-determining individuals in the pursuit of their self-chosen goals" (1993, p. 160). The fast-paced change is revolutionary and tolerated with a minority view that opposes modernization and reform. Institutions are redefined, communications and new technologies are flourishing, freedom of assembly and movement, private property rights and the promotion of a market economy are helping Afghanistan enter the age of globalization (Sedra & Middlebrook, 2004).

There are numerous women's rights organizations, the Afghan Independent Human Rights Commission, and over 200 free publications in the country. For the first time independent, private TV and radio stations have broken the traditional state monopoly over media (Tarzi, 2006). However, there are signs that conservatism and ultra-nationalism tendencies are on the rise but not yet strong enough to dictate change. As Tilly has aptly specified, under such circumstances in many democratizing societies, six fundamental assumptions can be drawn "1) democratization occurs... over years or decades; 2) prevailing circumstances under which democratization occurs vary significantly from era to era and region to region as a function of the international environment, available models of political organization and predominant patterns of social relations; 3) multiple paths to democracy exist; 4) most social environments...contain major obstacles to democracy; 5) yet such obstacles diminish rapidly under specifiable circumstances, and 6) democratization...still occurs rarely because... major political actors have strong incentives and means to block the very processes that promote democracy" (2002, p. 190). Tilly's assumptions can be applied to the present day case of Afghanistan, where democracy's path is far from clearly delineated. Its history illustrates numerous examples of how democratic reform has never taken hold and major political actors inside and outside of the country are working against the democratic process succeeding. Democracy could, indeed, take decades to take hold in this war-torn nation.

Afghan Women in Society

Twenty-three years of conflict – Soviet occupation, civil war, the Taliban, and finally the US-led bombing campaign – have taken a toll on women in Afghanistan (Hans, 2004). Throughout the 20th century, the debate on women's rights and their role in Afghan society has been closely interlinked with the national destiny. "Gender has thus been one of the most politicized issues in Afghanistan over the past 100 years, and attempts at reform have been denounced by opponents as un-Islamic and a challenge to the sanctity of the faith and family" (World Bank, 2004, xi). During the many years of turmoil, concerns about women's security led to the imposition of strict interpretations of socially acceptable female behavior, supported by the most conservative reading of Islamic scriptures. Afghan women suffered tremendously from human rights violations throughout the conflict. Today many still struggle against ongoing violence, abuse and life-threatening conditions in a post-conflict country wracked with problems (United Nations Development Fund for Women (UNIFEM), 2004).

Afghanistan has been ranked at the bottom of the United Nations Gender Development Index (2001) and the fifth poorest country in the world according to the United Nations Development Program Human Index Report (2004). The illiteracy rate for the country is estimated at 70 percent. Those rates hover around 96 percent for Afghan women in the rural areas. Though nearly five million children have returned to school since 2001, it is estimated that only 30 percent of girls are enrolled in primary schools (UNICEF, 2006).

Under the Taliban regime, women and girls over 8 years of age were forbidden from receiving an education, though many continued to study secretly in underground schools. Due to years of war and conflict, a large population of widows exists and over 500,000 Afghan women are heads of households (UNDP, 2002). The life expectancy of Afghan women living in Afghanistan or neighboring refugee camps is only 45 years, while for men it is only 47 years (U.S. Department of State, 2002). Afghanistan is one of the few countries where the life expectancy of men is longer than women's.

Afghanistan has one of the highest maternal mortality rates in the world at 1,600 deaths per 100,000 live births, with one woman dying of pregnancy-related complications every thirty minutes, and nearly 87 percent of those deaths preventable (World Health Organization, 2005). Seventy-Five percent of Afghan women lack essential maternal care due to the absence of health facilities, and cultural traditions preventing women from seeking medical care.

The statistics for raising children are equally grim. One quarter of all children die before reaching the age of five (UNICEF, 2004). Fifty percent of Afghan children suffer from chronic malnutrition, and 30 percent are orphans. The lack of education, health facilities, and basic needs for children leads to great emotional and psychological trauma among Afghan mothers.

When women have equal opportunities for education, employment, and health care, it will not only improve their own lives, but will likely have positive impacts on their families. This is where media and a constitutional-abiding democratic society can uphold ideals of equality and fair treatment for its citizens, promoting progressive change in all sectors of life in Afghan society. Media can communicate information crucial to its citizenry, helping to inform and educate the populace. In a country such as Afghanistan, where all infrastructures have been damaged or are lacking, media can be a mobilizing agent.

The Road Ahead for Afghan Women

After many years of living under oppressive rule, Afghan women are once again legally able to participate in society, whether in the work force, media or in politics, but not without personal sacrifice and occasional threats to their lives. The Afghan Independent Human Rights Commission complained in a report in March 2006 that Afghan women face discrimination and mistreatment that includes rape, murder, and forced marriages (Afghanistan Independent Human Rights Committee (AIHRC), 2006).

There are continued threats against Afghan women journalists, and the media sector is in peril of stricter regulations with the rise of fundamentalist Islamic elements in the parliament and ministries. In May 2005, Shaima Rezayee, a young female presenter of a popular music show on the privately owned Tolo TV, was found shot dead in her home in Kabul. Though two of her brothers were eventually arrested then released in this case, she had been heavily criticized by Islamic conservatives and her life threatened because of her Western broadcast style and association with the television show (Esfandiari, 2006).

40

This is a time of historical transformation for the Afghan people, and especially the women as they attempt to carve out a meaningful place for themselves in Afghan society.   The stakes are high. Without the presence of NATO peacekeeping forces and the US military, the fledgling Afghan government might not be able to stave off Islamic fundamentalist groups such as the Taliban, al-Qaeda, and renegade warlords who threaten the development of human rights and civil society. These groups still wield influence along the border regions of Afghanistan and Pakistan, and are battling to regain their stronghold.   1,600 people died in conflict-related violence in 2005, and estimates for 2006 hover near 4,000; clearly one of the bloodiest years since the fall of the Taliban (Integrated Regional Information Networks (IRIN), 2006). The fate of Afghan women is far from secure in such an environment.

Media Development

Of the many new developments gaining ground in Afghan society, media are emerging with great energy and dynamic force.   Print, radio, and television are thriving despite attempts to impose censorship and other oppressive measures by Islamic conservatives which threaten the freedom of the press guaranteed under the newly ratified Afghan Constitution (Ibrahimi, 2006). Under the Taliban regime and during the Soviet Occupation, the press was controlled by the state. Afghanistan enjoyed relative media freedom in the 1960's and late 1980's. Independent media began with the promulgation of the 1964 Afghan Constitution by King Mohammed Zahir (Rawan, 2002). That document ushered in what is commonly referred to as Afghanistan's "decade of democracy." The constitution decreed that "every Afghan has the right to express his thoughts in speech, in writing, in pictures, and by other means, in accordance with the provisions of the law" (Government of Afghanistan, 1964). The 1964 constitution further stated that every Afghan has the right to print

41

and publish ideas in accordance with the law without prior screening by state authorities.

The Afghan government soon promulgated the 1965 press law to regulate the media sector. It reiterated the constitutional guarantees, but forbade obscenity and any "matter implying defamation of the principles of Islam or defamatory to the King" (Razi, 1994) While broadcast media remained the prerogative of the state, the number of independent newspapers mushroomed under the new legal framework (Rawan, 2002).

The next media shake-up came in 1973, after Mohammad Daoud led a coup d'etat that ended the country's monarchical system. The result was nearly three decades of restrictions on a free media, culminating in the hard-line Taliban regime's crackdown until it was ousted by international intervention in late 2001 (Farivar, 1999).

From 1992 until late 2001, women were not allowed on television or represented in any form of media. They were considered non-citizens without any rights or power. Today, women are protected as equal citizens under the new constitution, and once again are being seen, heard and read about in the media. Activists estimate that there are about 1,000 women working throughout Afghanistan as journalists for radio, television, or print publications (Tarzi, 2006). The 2004 Afghan Constitution describes freedom of expression as "inviolable" and guaranteed to every Afghan in the form of "speech, writing, illustration, or other means" (Afghan Constitution, 2004). It explicitly prohibits the state from requiring a priori approval of "printed or published" materials. The constitution also seeks to avoid arbitrary limitations on the media. It states that directives related to the dissemination of information – whether in print or broadcast – will be "regulated by law" (Article 19 & Global Campaign for Free Expression, 2006).

Despite these protections, Afghan men and women in the field of media are struggling to maintain their freedom of expression and to carve out a voice for themselves[4]. President Karzai issued a decree setting out a new law on mass media in December 2005 – just days before the inauguration of the country's first directly elected legislature. However, the government's latest attempt to liberalize the media may come under attack from a parliament that is largely under the control of fundamentalist mujahideen, some of whom seem to have a poor grasp of the concept of press freedom. Despite the odd timing and the resulting ambiguity, the document could enable Afghanistan to become a democratic state with a fully functioning – and free – mass media (Eickelman & Anderson, 1999). However that depends on the strength of the yet untested press-freedom commitment of those interpreting and enforcing the new law. Currently, there are indications of a conservative backlash against the progressive strides which have been undertaken by the media over the past five years.

It has been emphasized in this chapter that Afghanistan has gone through nearly 25 years of conflict and upheaval which has had a catastrophic impact on the nation, especially affecting Afghan women and human rights. Media have played a progressive role in helping to shape modern Afghanistan, however they have been curtailed and controlled throughout various political chapters in Afghan society, and continue to be threatened by conservative factions in the country today (Reporters Sans Frontiers, 2006). This remains an ongoing battle in the political and social transformation of Afghanistan, evolving from a medieval mindset to a progressive path.

In the next chapter, first-hand accounts from interview subjects regarding the current transition to democracy in post-Taliban Afghanistan are explored and discussed. The role of the media, democratic reform, and emerging participation of Afghan women are addressed in this fragile process, and several themes and issues that were established in previous chapters are tested.

---

[4] The December 2005 release of a women's rights magazine editor from three months in jail after allegedly printing "un-Islamic" content in a few articles shows how tenuous freedom of the press is in modern-day Afghanistan (Article 19 & Global Campaign for Free Expression, 2006).

CHAPTER FOUR:

THE AFGHAN EXPERIENCE: VOICES ON THE GROUND

In this chapter the role that mass media play in promoting the development of democracy and civil society in a post-conflict nation such as Afghanistan will be explored through an analysis of first-hand accounts of interview subjects, all of whom are experts in their respective fields, regarding the current transition to democracy in post-Taliban Afghanistan[5]. Against this background civic participation and the evolving position of Afghan women within their society is considered. The analytical framework is provided by key themes set out in Chapter Two, namely, the role of the media; empowerment of women; and, civil society, freedom of the press, and human rights. The established experts will shed light on the current situation of media development, the status and changing role of Afghan women, and the challenges faced by emerging democracy in this war-torn nation.

Over the course of my interviewing, the discussion on the role of media in Afghanistan proved to be highly charged and dynamic. Resoundingly, the interview subjects felt that media play a very important and multi-faceted role within society, helping to raise awareness and educate the population, and at the same time expose new and different ideas that inevitably enact change over time, for example, the promotion of women's rights and civic participation, and the development and strengthening of civil society. In this manner, media, more specifically radio, television and print, are seen as a powerful agent of change and a mobilizing force.

---

[5] (See: Appendix III. All dates of interviews included in this section).

Media Development

As discussed in Chapter Three, the media under the Taliban regime and during the many years of war were restricted and state-controlled, and completely male-dominated (Farivar, 1999). Media development has really only occurred since 2002, and according to Afghan Ambassador to Canada, Omar Samad, who as a former government spokesperson personally witnessed media growth after the fall of the Taliban in Afghanistan:

> This new phase is only four years old, but the strides have been remarkable and unbelievable in many ways. In the past four years I have experienced and I have witnessed a whole new generation of young Afghan men and women who are now media savvy, and themselves producers of media content and programming. People who never ever had any training or education in these fields, who are now very creative and very courageous, are promoting freedom of expression in Afghanistan.

On this same point, Jane McElhone, the former project director for the Institute for Media, Policy, and Civil Society (IMPACS), a Canadian NGO focused on training women journalists, found that the media environment in Afghanistan was rapidly developing during her three years there.

> There was so much else happening, so I think there was a drive to work with the Afghans to get the media institutions going and to train the journalists so that they could cover the reconstruction process so as much as possible people in Afghanistan could participate in it, talk

about it, could give their opinions about it, and could understand what was going on around them.

It was important to get women involved from the onset of the training process as well, to be involved and have them be seen as an integral part of what was evolving around them. The fact that people started seeing women again on the air telling stories, heard them on the radio, and read their stories in newspapers and magazines was a critical component for Afghan society to accept Afghan women working in the media in such a public manner. One should not forget that just five years ago, Afghan women were forbidden in the media and from participation in almost all aspects of public life.

According to Ms. McElhone, "conditioning is the first step to acceptance." The fact that people heard women talking about issues made it, "(A) seem more normal for women to be part of the process, and (B) for the women who were listening at home they saw that it was possible for women to be out in the media, to be public, and to be talking." This offers the potential to serve as a role model for other women to observe and possibly follow, and potentially conveys a message to encourage and empower women's civic participation in the reconstruction efforts of their country.

Saad Mohseni, the Founder and Director of TOLO TV and ARMAN FM, the first commercial television and radio station in Afghanistan's history, vocalized a similar viewpoint, stating that media provide a platform where women can have a voice again, and that media help dissolve gender and ethnicity boundaries. "Once members of the Afghan public see a woman for the umpteenth time talking about an issue they stop seeing that person as a woman or a man or a Hazara or a Tajik or a Pashtun[6]. He or she sees them as a politician, a commentator, or a writer; sees them as a true professional." It is through the power of media's exposure that boundaries

---

[6] Hazara, Tajik and Pashtun refer to various ethnic groups in Afghanistan (Dupree, 1977).

potentially can be eradicated and viewpoints changed, especially in a country such as Afghanistan where illiteracy and conservative cultural norms threaten progress.

World institutions such as the United Nations recognize that an encouraging development has been the revival of women's roles in journalism and the media since the overthrow of the Taliban. "More than 20 newspapers have been launched by and for women in Kabul and several women's radio stations have gone on the air in the capital and the provinces" (Kandiyoti, 2005, p. 28), providing a focus and "a political voice to women journalists" who have added their efforts to shaping public opinion in the crucial debates on the future of Afghanistan.

On the Empowerment of Women

A common point that arose over and over again in the interviews was the belief that media helped to empower Afghan women by providing them a public presence once again after so many years of oppression and seclusion from public space. Peter Erben, the former Chief Electoral Officer of the Joint Electoral Management Body, who was in charge of organizing and implementing the Parliamentary and Provincial Council Elections for Afghanistan in September 2005, asserted that:

> Media absolutely empower women in Afghan society today, especially in public campaigning processes where it is more acceptable for men to participate, so it can be difficult for women to campaign in Afghanistan. Media, especially in the 2005 elections, gave women the opportunity to campaign via media by giving them free access to campaign. How much the actual impact is very hard to ascertain or measure, but the fact is that Afghan women in very large numbers seized the opportunity to go and report their campaign messages and get them out.

Media have often been viewed as a champion for women's rights and a supporter of their civic participation in society. However, according to Lacey (1996), women's position within media power structures and media representation of women are persistent concerns in every society, because negative stereotyping and lack of female input both reflect and reinforce wide gender inequalities.

Dr. Sima Samar, the Director of the Afghan Independent Human Rights Commission, and former Minister of Women's Affairs in Afghanistan, firmly believed that, "there is no doubt that media has played a very big role in exposing every issue in the country. And, the cause of the Afghan women was brought outside the country through the media, otherwise, during the Taliban times and even before, Afghanistan was a really closed country; there was not much news coming out from inside." She continued to elaborate, stressing that:

> We should not forget that specifically with women's issues media created a lot of international solidarity for the Afghan women. Especially when the Taliban announced its policies against women, putting so many restrictions on their lives, and at first the situation was not taken very seriously until it was picked up by the international media and made into an issue.

Media clearly play an important role in disseminating information that society needs to find out about, helping to raise awareness about critical issues, and influencing change.

Rina Amiri, a former Political Officer for UNAMA and special advisor to the SRSG (Special Representative of the Secretary General) in Kabul, Afghanistan, agreed with Dr. Samar, saying that, "media have played a very important role, both international and local media." However, local media need more support, and with the launch of the Afghan Women Journalists' Forum in 2002, funded by UNIFEM and USAID under the auspices of the "Strengthening Information, Media and Communication in Afghanistan" program, Afghan women journalists have found a support network at the local level which provides them with training and experience (Kandiyoti, 2005). As for international media, she continued:

> We can go back to the period of the Taliban where the greatest area of scrutiny was the area of women's rights in Afghanistan, and the travesty of the way women were being treated. The international media really focused on the devastating situation of women, and I think that created a certain level of self-consciousness among Afghan society, and surely within Afghanistan, as well as among the Afghan Diaspora. Certainly within Afghanistan there is a keen awareness that the international community saw Afghanistan as a place that was extremely oppressive towards women.

Ms. Amiri stated that in her opinion both local and international media have played a critical role in raising awareness about gender-dynamics in the country, and that awareness has improved the situation for women to some extent. Media may or may not be a facilitator of women's empowerment; however, according to Sakr (2004), media have provided channels of communication whereby women have been able to 'voice' their concerns and needs to a public that previously had neither exposure nor access to these hidden matters.

Clementina Cantoni, the former Project Director for the Helping Afghan Widows Assistance program (HAWA) run by CARE International in Kabul, Afghanistan, stated that in her opinion the local media also helped to promote and expose women within Afghan society. She noted that during the three years she worked in Afghanistan, "there was definitely a change in how openly and more visible women were. I think it was more tangible; more women were out, going to work. Just the fact that you could see more women's faces was exciting. And, you could see them on Afghan television."

However, a commonality that came up again and again in the interviews was the serious challenges continuing to face Afghan women, especially the obstacles preventing them from participating as equal members of society. This sentiment was expressed by Mr. Erben when he said, "Afghan women are without doubt, some of the most challenged women in the world because they live in a society that still has an incredibly long way to go, without any measurement of equality between men and women."

There is no doubt that there are still significant challenges for Afghan women to overcome before they can reach any type of reasonable participation in Afghan society. These interview subjects' opinions, although optimistic, clearly express concern about the future course for Afghan women. It is very difficult to measure levels of empowerment of women in any sense, let alone through the media. However, one of the clearest messages to be derived from various studies and attempts at analyzing women's empowerment in the media has been that most voices are stifled, especially in non-western societies, and that women's voices are stifled worst of all (Sakr, 2004). Unless there is more equal participation of men and women in public platforms such as media and politics, Afghan society will continue to suffer from an unhealthy imbalance and lack of communicative action and civic participation from its citizenry.

Importance of Education

Grant Kippen, the former Country Director for NDI (National Democratic Institute), and former Chair for the Electoral Complaints Commission in Kabul, Afghanistan, argues that media empower women by covering women's issues and their reactions to those issues. However, he is not as clear on how 'empowered' Afghan women actually are at this point in time. A common finding shared by all the interview subjects is the importance placed on education for a country such as Afghanistan with an illiteracy rate of 70 percent (UNDP, 2004).

Dahlgren (2000) stresses that education is crucial for a healthy democracy because literacy is essential for democratic citizenry. Mr. Kippen added:

> The biggest challenge across the board right now in Afghanistan is education. Specifically, with relation to media, it's educating media in how to cover issues and events, and maybe there is a natural bias towards men, but I think it's only in educating the media and the broader population as well that women have a role to play here.

However, he agreed that any attention is good because "it helps drive up the awareness of others."

Ms. McElhone agreed with several other interviewees that media need to be properly educated to cover important issues and bring credibility to their coverage:

> As Afghans are assuming greater control over their own future, the journalists have to keep on par with what is going on in the political level and on every other level to maintain credibility. They have such a learning curve to go through. Many of the journalists are very young, immature and uneducated; not sophisticated. Journalists have to keep the population informed about what is going on, and journalists can play a huge role in bringing about transparency and ensuring accountability. It's so important. If the quality isn't there, if the journalists are not credible, then that creates a big problem with the public. Especially in a country that doesn't have a great history of independent media.

Ambassador Samad also stressed that education for journalists and the media needed strengthening. To this end, several new journalism programs have been developed at a handful of universities throughout the country to tackle this problem. However, assistance from the international media in this area would also be of great benefit to helping develop the fledgling Afghan media.

Ms. Rasekh added that creating effective programming in a post-conflict society such as Afghanistan is critical, because people really need to be educated. "Entertainment is good to have, but in a country like Afghanistan we need a lot of educational programs, programs that heal people in post-conflict situations."

Mr. Mohseni put the same stress on the importance of accountability, and that media play an important role in this regard. Initially, he saw the role of media as providing entertainment to an entertainment hungry public. However, that role has changed dramatically over the last four years.

> In particular in relation to issues like accountability and balancing how things are communicated to the public. By accountability I mean that we have no justice system, there's not much police control, and the public is exceptionally frustrated by the way things are handled domestically by the government. The media balances things in terms of if people are not informed at least they are exposed. If issues are not discussed by the government, at least there's a place in the media where people can air their frustrations and their grievances. At the same time, people get the other side of the story.

He stressed that media provide balance in this manner, and help to educate and inform the public offering them the complete story; "therefore, I think the role of the media in Afghanistan is a lot bigger than it might be in most other places." Media industries play a pivotal role in organizing the images and discourse through which people make sense of the world. Public exposure of injustices can serve to break the cycle by which "social and economic inequality reinforces political inequality" (Barnett, 2003). Effectively used, channels of media communication can promote a "politics of shame", whereby societal issues and promises can be monitored and held accountable. In a country like Afghanistan, where human rights still suffer and the justice system is in need of serious reform, the media can help by shining a light on injustices, mobilizing the public to act.

Too Much Change Too Fast?

Zohra Rasekh, the Director of the International Women's Affairs and Human Rights Department at the Ministry of Foreign Affairs in Kabul, Afghanistan, stated that media have come a long way in the past four years, and have shown great signs of improvement. She has witnessed:

> Advocacy for improving the situation of women; violence against women has been addressed; there have been some campaigns through the media, some awareness-raising. You see more women appearing on television as broadcasters or announcers, even once in a while they invite women to speak about their issues and problems. The whole mentality in the entire country is being challenged. I personally think this is good, however if we do more than what is being done it may backfire. Those who have the Taliban mentality, they're not ready to see more women in radio, print or television, they may cause problems. It's good to do it slowly but surely.

Ambassador Samad echoed this same sentiment, stating that if Afghan society is pushed too hard too fast things might backfire as they have done repeatedly in recent Afghan history:

> We have to be thoughtful and, in my opinion, wise about how we implement change, and what kind of change we implement, and what

53

kind of timeline we implement it in. How do we first prepare the people for the changes that will take place? Occasionally, it's good to inject quick change, and other times it's better to inject it gradually over time because it's a fragile situation, it's a fragile democracy, it's not a completely secure environment, not a stable environment. There are a lot of other things that are at stake if we go too far.

For example, several journalists and editors have been threatened, jailed, or killed within the last couple of years by conservative elements within the country who are threatened by what they see as un-Islamic traditions and Western cultural norms being introduced into society (Esfandiari, 2006; Ibrahimi, 2006).

Ms. Rasekh admitted that, "some of the edicts – even the freedom of speech legalized in the Constitution – have been threatened" by conservative elements in the country. In trying to support women in the media one or two of the private television stations have received threats and some of their journalists have been harassed. Ms. Amiri expanded her thoughts about media's role in Afghanistan:

Having worked with the UN, I have always seen the media as quite helpful in a monitoring role and an advocacy role. By shedding light on some issues, by exposing certain issues, it forces people to respond and react. By putting that level of scrutiny out there, it makes key agents, whether the UN or the Afghan government, take more concrete action to address shortcomings; in a way it forces them to become responsive. And, in that regard I think that the media has done a good job.

Barnett (2003) states that "media exposure remains a crucial resource for pressuring powerful institutions to act in accord with publicly accepted norms rather than from narrow private interest" (p. 65), and in fulfilling these responsibilities media reflect the "watchdog" role that Norris (2000) describes in *A Virtuous Circle*. Several of the interview subjects echo these sentiments in their own opinions, noting that media help to force the powers that be in Afghanistan to own up to their responsibilities in taking action where needed, preventing as many injustices from slipping under the radar.

On Role Models

Another common response was on the importance of role models, and how media help create Afghan women role models, either working within the media or in politics. All of the interview subjects commented on this aspect, stating that it was a significant development for both Afghan women and men to witness, and would undoubtedly help bring about social change in the country.

Ms. Amiri shared that:

> By having educated women, and women represented in the media who are delivering messages with a lot of substance, that is helping reshape perceptions of women's capacities and women's potential roles in society. Certainly, having those women icons out there, and Afghan women journalist icons out there, is certainly challenging these stereotypes, and is very important for society as a whole. Within the political domain, both women and men in the media are honing in on women, giving them the ability and providing them the capacity to profile women leaders. You see that more and more in parliament, women are playing quite a prominent role.

According to a recent United Nations report on gender and reconstruction in Afghanistan, more challenges lay in wait concerning the level of participation and representation of women in Afghan society (Kandiyoti, 2005). Though the report acknowledges positive strides by Afghan women, especially in the parliament, it also states that there needs to be more "creative ways of engaging with male community leaders and elders so as to ensure that provisions for women's rights to political participation can translate from principle to reality" (Kandiyoti, p. 29). Though media are certainly viewed as helpful and supportive in certain circumstances, especially in calling attention to the status of Afghan women and encouraging their civic participation, gaps may exist between perception and reality as noted by several of the interview subjects.

Roya Rahmani, the Project Director for Rights and Democracy, a Canadian NGO focused on developing women's rights in Afghanistan, stated that media are a very good means of transferring education and knowledge because in a very conservative society, it is not easy to get people to change. In her opinion, media provide a very neutral medium, and are one of the best ways to transfer knowledge and education:

> For example, by seeing a woman speaking in the Parliament or a woman as an anchor on TV, this builds confidence in women's talents that have been missing for a long period of time. 85 percent of the Afghan population is still living in the rural areas with limited access to what is going on. However, by having access to radio and television, they are exposed to a lot of good programs that are targeting various issues. They offer role models and even role play, showing families working problems out, women participating, etc. This is very important information dissemination. Media provides an educational role, helping to increase knowledge and awareness about many issues.

The same UN report acknowledges the strengths of media support in post-conflict Afghanistan as well as the recent increase in women's involvement within the media and political sectors. However, it is quick to point out that "whether the inclusion of women will represent a genuine challenge to the existing political culture of Afghanistan will need to be evaluated in the light of developments on the ground" (Kandiyoti, 2005). The author of the report points to the more daunting task of securing women's fundamental rights to education and health over their civic and political participation as critical factors to the ongoing reconstruction of the country. Several of the interview subjects agreed with this perspective, stating that basic human requirements such as nutrition, housing, medical care and education needed to be established for the majority of Afghan women over concerns for political and social rights.

Ms. McElhone states that the Afghan women in the public eye are really pioneers in what they are accomplishing: testing the public limits, either in media or politics; testing their family and society limits; talking about women's issues publicly, getting them on the agenda; and, eventually, influencing public policy.

> It is so important to have Afghan women role models especially for
> the younger generation growing up, and also for women in general
> who lived under the Taliban. Again, if the media is doing their job
> and using their mandate to make sure that women are used as sources
> for quotations and that women are working in the media, and that
> women who are out in political life are being covered in the media,
> then I think that there will be a lot of good, future role models for
> Afghan women.

Ambassador Samad developed this sentiment further by stating that:

> The media can help, the media can be a vehicle for them, and I believe
> that not only are these pioneering women role models for others, but
> overall they are actually building the foundation of a new country -
> whether it's building the economic foundation, or societal foundation,

or political foundation – now they feel that they are part of this change, and that's the way is should be. Media helps them accomplish this task, and visa versa they help media get this message out, and they allow media and provide media with new ideas. So, it's a two-way street.

Clearly, the majority of the interview subjects feel very strongly that media are a significant force in helping to enact change within Afghan society, by not only providing a platform for Afghan women to express themselves but also by encouraging them to become active participants, thereby leading by example and becoming important role models for other women and girls.

Ms. Cantoni had a very personal experience to share about women's empowerment in the media as well as the importance of role models. In her opinion, she shared that not only does media help create role models, but it also promotes the whole concept of women's participation in the country's affairs for the first time after many, many years, sending a powerful message to the rest of the community, especially to the rest of the women in the community. Ms. Cantoni was kidnapped and held hostage in Kabul for 26 days in May and June 2005, and thankfully released unharmed. Her personal story received international media attention. In Ms. Cantoni's view:

The media has an incredible effect on women's empowerment. Certainly in regards to my own case when I was held hostage the fact that these women were filmed protesting, displaying their anger and grief, to me was a victory definitely for the women. Because finally the world was taking notice of this huge sector of society, which until that moment had been largely ignored or not considered very much and certainly not listened to. It's a shame that they were noticed for a cause that really is not a relevant one, but I hope that in some way the fact that they did gain a voice sensitized people to their plight. Mine was secondary in the bigger picture.

Ms. Cantoni's plight became international news, invoking pleas from President Karzai to Pope Benedict XVI for her safe release. However, this unique situation does not reflect the ongoing reality and challenges that Afghan women continue to face. According to Bathla (1998), "media has rendered insignificance to women's voices and conveyed that their concerns are irrelevant to democratic polity thus also indicating that a free press in itself cannot guarantee representation of opinions and values of marginalized sections" (p. 109). Indeed, society as a whole needs to bring about key changes in cultural norms and attitudes towards women's participation otherwise the changes will either be superficial or negligible over time. Media is a mobilizing force but can only help to bring about so much change; the onus is on society itself.

On How Media Helps to Promote Civil Society

Ambassador Samad notes that as part of the new Afghanistan that has emerged since late 2001, the whole process of democratization and political change has accompanied other types of changes, namely, in economic progress and security issues. However, he stated that the emergence of civil society is probably more important than anything else in the long run, because the components that make up civil society include issues that make up human rights, women's rights, and freedom of the press. All of these components have to be rooted in and supported by a legal system. This system has to be understood, and be interpreted and conveyed to the Afghan population so they can understand what it means. However, it is not something that can be done overnight and it will take a long time. Media play a special role in disseminating this important information, along with educating the public.

Ambassador Samad stated that the media are very important not only in introducing change but helping to shape changes within society, and that civil society requires a strong media presence in order to fulfill its own responsibilities to the public. He continued to say that:

> If there is an issue that has to do with human rights, the fastest, best, most efficient way to convey that to the public is through the media. It's obviously a give and take relationship – a marriage of convenience – one where they need each other to perform well. The growth and maturity of civil society over time and that of the media are very much inter-related.

Ms. Cantoni agreed. In her opinion, she noted that where there was a good, strong journalism tradition, civil society and human rights were in fact protected and promoted by the media[7].

> When programs or journalists go and uncover stories, or try and give voice to people who didn't previously have one, then media has a fundamental role in establishing civil society. Particularly, in opening debates, looking at potentially controversial subjects, but allowing freedom of expression. It's fundamental, and it's something that was not allowed for many years in Afghanistan so it very new now.

That newness and lack of experience also contributes to a weaker media, more prone to flaws and errors.

Mr. Erben felt that media have a long way to go to "provide a free and fair media in Afghanistan." In specific relation to promoting civic participation and

---

[7] See: Reporters Sans Frontiers (2006).

women's rights, he expressed concern that the media lacked development and experience in this arena, and at times had a detrimental effect on the electoral process through imbalanced reporting.

> Media still has a long way to go to play a positive role in promoting Afghan women's participation in political life in Afghanistan. Obviously, media is important, because if there is one way in which women can get an opportunity to speak out and get their opinions out there without putting themselves in direct confrontation with men it is through the media. I still believe that there is a long way to go for media to help promote Afghan women in society.

And, he added that media needs to learn how to report more responsibly and accurately. "Hearing both sides of the story is still something that needs to be developed in Afghanistan."

On Freedom of the Press

Ms. McElhone stated that it is very important to push the boundaries of society in order to enact change. However, it is just as important to realize to which degree society has evolved, and are willing and ready to accept new changes and ideas. She is a staunch advocate of press freedom and freedom of expression. However in a country like Afghanistan these freedoms do not come without challenges or a cost.

> Despite all the challenges and poverty facing Afghanistan, there is still a level of press freedom. There are countries that are in far worse media situations that have had far more opportunities. However, there are certain subjects that remain taboo and a whole handful of elected officials and warlords who still wield strong influence in society that

put pressure on the media. Those issues have to be made public, however it is a fine line that you walk but you need to test the boundaries. If nobody is willing to test the boundaries, the boundaries will never widen or change. You always need to push them but keep an eye on what is happening around you.

She also argued that the bigger problem appears to be self-censorship among Afghan journalists, stating that many practice self-censorship in order to avoid dealing with authority figures that will undoubtedly come after them if they dare question taboo or religious topics within Afghan society (Tarzi, 2006).

Ms. Amiri said that in her opinion the media play a very important role in ensuring freedom and promoting human rights in Afghanistan, and that in comparison to its neighboring countries, such as Pakistan and Iran, it is seen as a relatively open society.

Part of it is because there has been a real focus in allowing and encouraging freedom of the press, and that the international community has worked closely with the Afghan government to ensure that freedom of the press remains a key principle that's respected and promoted. Allowing the media to have a prominent role creates a system of checks and balances, allows a certain level of scrutiny, and a level of open debate.

She continued to say that the level of open debate witnessed today has never existed in Afghanistan, and reflects a plurality of voices that are conveyed through the media, debating political and cultural issues.

The level of openness among the media has been very important towards potentially opening up the process and creating a more healthy and dynamic society in Afghanistan. According to Ms. Amiri, if that element were absent from the media a very different process would be in place today. The international community would have less of a perception that a democratic system has been placed in Afghanistan. Certainly elections are important and people recognize that it is an inclusive process that needs to be in place, but the focus is on the level of openness in society – the ability to challenge, to question, to confront – the key power holders and the government. The media represent that that right exists in the country, and that it definitely is a crucial part of the development of democracy in Afghanistan. She added that, "the one thing that has allowed the media to develop has been the continued support of the international media and its advocacy for freedom of the press, for those principles to be in place."

Mr. Mohseni stated that in his opinion freedom of the press and freedom of expression are two of Afghanistan's greatest achievements since the fall of the Taliban. He pointed to the development of hundreds of publications, half a dozen private television stations, and dozens of radio stations as "the pride and joy of the international community", and the envy of the region and the Muslim world.

However, these tenets of democracy have not come without a price or major challenges, and more specifically in relation to Mr. Mohseni's stations, his journalists, his family, and his own life have been threatened by those who want to limit these freedoms. He explained:

> Freedom of the press, this is a very, very important issue, but it's a tug of war. I think that every country, even in the US, there's a tug of war; for example, between the pro- and anti-Bush media. I think it's a tug of war that never ends. The media always fights for the rights to express itself, and the government always tries to limit the media's freedom in terms of how it expresses itself. It's a bit like "you can say anything you want as long as it's pro-government", a statement that

has echoed throughout different capital cities. That's a battle that we expected, and we are expecting to fight for a long, long time.

The battle for freedom of the press and freedom of expression exists all over the world, and is not a unique case in Afghanistan. Ironically, in our post-9/11 world there seems to be an even larger battle to uphold these tenets and resist attempts at censorship and government control of the media. The battle rages in Eastern and Western hemispheres, and reveals no signs of dissipating in the near future.

On Human Rights

Ms. Amiri stated that:

In terms of women's rights certainly the political process has allowed for a core leadership within women's organizations and allowed for women leaders to emerge. But, at the same time if you look outside of Kabul, if you look at the lives of the vast majority of women, I would say that to a large extent that their situation still remains unchanged. The human rights situation in the country continues to be of serious concern, and the level of poverty that exists in the country to a large extent has not changed over the last 4.5 years.

Ms. Rahmani expressed a similar opinion:

A conservative and uneducated society like Afghanistan is not easy to change. These changes are not going to happen overnight, not after so many years of war and cultural restrictions which were imposed. With the various challenges such as education, access to resources, and the very corrupt judicial and legal system, these aspects have a direct impact on women and human rights in the country.

According to the first ever National Human Development Report (2004) put out by the UNDP, poverty, unemployment and inequality are "bigger threats to the everyday lives of Afghans than traditional security threats" (p. 34), which definitely puts the human rights picture into a much sharper perspective when considering the many elements at play in Afghanistan.

Ms. Amiri elaborated by saying that the human rights situation in certain places of the country was very grave and quite atrocious. Part of the reason is the lack of rule of law because the central government is not able to extend its decree beyond the urban centers in the country, and no checks and balance system that deals with security and various issues exists throughout the country. Ms. Amiri did not think that the last four and a half years has done much with regard to improving the situation of women, or the overall human rights situation, "certainly not from what I have observed from monitoring certain human rights cases in various parts of the country."

Mr. Mohseni said that through the power of media's exposure, actions or the lack of actions of a people or government lead to consequences. In this manner, media help keep people honest, by continuing to uncover aspects trying to get "at the truth." He added that, "of course, the media will always question if things are not being handled the right way, the media will question what has gone wrong, and why things are not being done properly." Additionally, by giving "honest figures within society a voice," this provided a very important and necessary function, especially in a country like Afghanistan where many believe they still live in a very unjust society. Again, media takes on its "watchdog" role, calling attention to injustices, mobilizing the public to act, and creating a public forum within which open discussions and deliberation can take place.

The Path to Democracy

Ms. Rasekh stated that both local and international media have an important role and responsibility in introducing and explaining the concept of democracy to the Afghan people. She expressed concern that one has to be very careful in advocating democracy because the concept is not yet clear, and it has possible negative connotations as a Western phenomenon with too much freedom associated with disrespectful behavior. "The definition of democracy for a lot of people inside the country seems to be not respecting the law, "I want to do whatever, and no one can tell me anything" kind of attitude." In this regard, Ms. Rasekh felt that media played an integral role in clarifying what democracy means, especially within an Islamic country like Afghanistan, where concepts such as freedom of expression or freedom of speech have no historical or cultural bearing.

Mr. Kippen echoed a similar point of view, and voiced concern that the concept of democracy had not been discussed or explained to the Afghan populace.

> People in Afghanistan have not had any discussion about what democracy means to them, what form of democracy they want, that hasn't trickled down to the district and local levels. People just don't understand it at this point in time. We talked earlier about education, and they really need to get at that. Illiteracy really impedes the ability to have those kinds of discussions.

Mr. Erben agreed that illiteracy as well as lack of media access were impediments to a successful electoral process. Additionally, he felt that the two critical factors of security and rule of law needed vast improvement throughout the country, and that democracy would only thrive in a stable environment. "Those are the two top priorities for Afghanistan to even embark on a path toward democracy – increased security and a solid system of rule of law. Without having a stable society it's very difficult to create a functional democracy in the country." Dahlgren's perspective on democracy underscores the viewpoints of these interview subjects when he states, "Democracy will not function if such virtues as tolerance and willingness to follow democratic principles and procedures do not have grounding in everyday life....Democracy will not survive a situation of profound lawlessness" (2000, p. 337). Afghanistan has a long way to go until a transparent system of good governance, legal reform and justice finds its way into society. What impact this will have on emerging democracy in this war-torn nation has yet to be established.

Dr. Samar said that what was still needed in order to facilitate the path to democracy was "respect for human rights and human dignity. And, specifically, women should not be counted as second-class citizens." However, in order to achieve these important aspects of a healthy civil society, Dr. Samar felt that several factors needed to be addressed and attained; namely, security throughout the country, "because without security we cannot reach anything, we cannot reconstruct the country. We cannot have democracy, and we cannot have human rights, or respect for human rights or dignity." Her perspective echoes the previous points of view, including that of Dahlgren and other deliberative democracy theorists who stress literacy, education and a strong respect for rule of law as laying the foundations for democracy.

Can Democracy take hold in Afghanistan?

When asked if democracy can really exist in a country like Afghanistan, Dr. Samar responded, "Why not? It depends on how much commitment we have among the Afghan people and international community to bring democracy to our country. Because we are not the only player; it's a globalized world." She added that the concept and words of democracy have to become real for the Afghan people in order to accept them.

Mr. Kippen stated that it would take successive generations and elections for democracy to take hold in Afghanistan because the concepts are still so new and foreign. He also said that a myth was created after the Bonn Agreement of 2001 that elections had to take place in the war-torn country, and that many in the international community equated elections with proof of democracy taking hold in Afghanistan (United Nations Assistance Mission to Afghanistan (UNAMA), 2001). He did not agree with this perspective.

> As long as we in the international community don't try to come in with models and impose what we think is the correct way to go then we stand a chance, or at least Afghanistan stands a chance. The biggest thing to me is that Afghans understand that they need to take ownership and responsibility for the process, and it can't be something that somebody else holds. If they see that through and through they are making the decisions, and they have to take the consequences of their actions from the decisions they make then it's a good chance that democracy, in some form or another will take hold.

This perspective is mirrored in several United Nations and world institution reports, cautioning unrealistic expectations about democracy taking hold in Afghanistan[8]. "There is a problematic disjuncture between, on the one hand, the time frames adopted and outputs expected by the international actors", who are driving various agendas, "and on the other, the length of time required for non-cosmetic changes in societal relations to begin to take shape" (Kandiyoti, 2005, p. 31). Unless great care is taken to local needs and priorities, this disjuncture may produce "unintended consequences that may prove detrimental" (p. 31).

---

[8] See: UNDP (2004), The World Bank (2005).

Ms. Rasekh asserted that democracy can be introduced and adopted in Afghanistan through education, through awareness-raising by media efforts, and through bringing in good models being used in other Islamic countries:

I think that will really help in bringing democracy into Afghanistan and maintaining it. It's good to see what other countries have done, looking at other models, and then implement…however, it will take a long time, at least a decade to build a democratic society.

Ms. Amiri agreed:

We have taken the first baby steps towards putting a democratic process in place. But, the real essence that needs to be in place, in terms of democratic institutions, in terms of a government that truly is representative, which addresses the needs of the country, one that responds to the views of the people, much more needs to be done.

Ms. Amiri added that the skeleton of the peace process had been put in place, but this process needed to be fleshed out and would take at least another ten years to accomplish. "We need all hands on deck to make sure that this doesn't become a peace process that works for 5 or so years, and then it falls apart. I think that we are still in danger of that happening. We certainly need to keep our commitment to Afghanistan at this time."

The National Development Framework, which was developed by the Afghan Government in cooperation with the UN in 2002, states that in order for true progress to take hold in the country, "(We) have to engage in a societal dialogue to enhance the opportunities of women and improve cooperation between men and women on the basis of our culture, the experience of other Islamic countries, and the global norms of human rights" (Government of Afghanistan, 2002: 13). These are wise words but how attainable a goal remains to be seen.

The Future Role of Afghan Women

When asked about the future role of Afghan women, in particular regard to the reconstruction of their country, all of the interview subjects expressed confidence in the growing role of women's participation in the political environment, specifically within the new Afghan Parliament which convened for the first time after nearly 30 years in January 2006. Afghan women parliamentarians were regarded as "agents of change" and "agents of peace," without blood on their hands from former participation in the many years of conflict (Coleman & Hunt, 2006).

Mr. Erben stated that women could play a very positive and powerful role in the national assembly, and that women's groups could introduce new ideas and values into Afghan society that had been previously eradicated. "If I was being forced to point out a specific area where women can play an important role it would certainly be there, where they can change some of the value systems that have been in place during civil war, and maybe introduce some new values into society in general, in the national assembly in particular."

Likewise, Mr. Kippen expressed a similar point of view, stating that culture, traditions, and attitudes can change, but they will take a long time to evolve:

I think there is an enormous opportunity for women that are in the Wolesi Jirga (National Assembly), and in the provincial councils to a certain extent. What I mentioned earlier about representation, and demonstrating your value as an elected representative, in my experience in Afghanistan, the women were the dynamic ones, they made things happen. So, there is an enormous opportunity there to step in and say 'well, where there is a problem here, we got it resolved.

In his opinion, there is a higher percentage of success for Afghan women acting in leadership roles than Afghan men, noticing that old ethnic and tribal alliances were starting to play out again in parliament, and that women had an opportunity to work outside of those structures.

Dr. Samar asserted that Afghan women make up more than half of the population, and they needed to be part of everything – policy making, and the implementation of policies. She was not in favor of a symbolic show of women's status in Afghanistan, but stressed that they should participate in the decision-making positions of the country:

> There should be more women participating, absolutely. We need to build upon the capacity of women in the country. We need more capacity-building in every field, especially after 25 years of war. They absolutely put us out during 25 years of war; we were not able to participate in society during that time. Everybody was interested in the men who hold a gun. Now, women can be seen as agents of peace. And, women should play a role in peace-building, and they should be at the negotiation table.

Ms. Amiri echoed a similar viewpoint, stating that when women are given the resources, when they are given the training, they have the capacity of serving as leaders, whether at the community level or international level. In her opinion:

> What would be important is to develop a strategy to find a way to broaden that level of training, broaden the level of resources, so that many more women across the country can benefit and take part in reconstruction efforts in Afghanistan, not just the same pool of women in Kabul. We have to figure out how to ensure that women become mainstream in all development work; that is going to be a priority over the next five years.

71

Ms. Rasekh thought that Afghan women's participation in politics and the parliament was a good start, but it was not enough to change the vast majority of women's lives throughout the country:

Unless we have a good, sound justice system and the rule of law, the situation of women is not going to change much. Even 25 percent representation of women in the parliament, or a few more women in the government does not mean that the situation of Afghan women has improved. It's good for the elite and those Afghan women lucky to be living in the cities, but we have a long way to go to change the situation of women in Afghanistan.

She felt that women could play an important role in various aspects of reconstruction, development, and the rebuilding of the country, but, the majority of women were still kept at home, out of the pubic life, and busy with the domestic side of existence.

Ms. Rasekh saw a glimmer of hope because:

Women have not been part of the conflict, have not planned the war, or are thinking about how to wage war; they have a better vision for the country, and they can plan better for peace and reconstruction. They are focusing on how to have peace and how to rebuild, and how to heal from all these years of war.

According to a recent UNRISD report, issues of gender equity and women's rights in Afghanistan will only be meaningfully addressed in the context of "multiple transitions" when there is a transition from "conflict and insecurity to peace, a political transition to a legitimate and effective state, and a socioeconomic transition to sustainable economic growth" (Kandiyoti, 2005, p. 31). Significant obstacles need to be overcome for the promises of reconstruction and national consolidation to materialize for women. Right now there are still major gaps between reality and hopeful goals put to paper. These changes will take time, perhaps a generation, to take hold in this country.

Ms. McElhone stated that there are obviously many negative examples that can be provided about media, but in Afghanistan she witnessed good examples where media can have an impact on community policy, how communities deal with issues, and how media can empower women in society and politics. In this regard, she notes there is a very clear link between media and politics.

An area where media can have a positive impact on empowering women in political life is where many women who live terribly isolated lives do not have access to education or information. Here, media can be an educational tool, helping to provide useful information for women's civic participation. Media can be a very effective tool in teaching women about the political process, even on the basic level of encouraging them to get out and vote. Though these are only individual actions, these actions eventually lead them to having a greater voice. Media's basic job is to ensure that people have as much information as possible to make effective choices about their own society and the future of their own country.

According to Calsamiglia (1999), "one of the most relevant sources of power today is information. Information allows people to make good choices. People who do not have access to information are discriminated in a way similar to those denied the vote a century ago. Without information, people choose irrationally. This is one reason that education is so important" (p. 137) and why media serve as a powerful force and mobilizing agent, especially in post-conflict Afghanistan, spreading news, information and acting as an educational tool.

Mr. Mohseni agreed that Afghan women's role were becoming more prominent, however felt that it was going to take a long time before women were on equal footing with men in Afghanistan. Even though the media to a large extent shone a spotlight on Afghan women within the media and the political arena, he did not think this was an accurate representation of women's participation around the country, and, ultimately:

> You have to let women come out and fight their own battles. And, you cannot impose this on Afghan society. We need women leaders and prominent women to come out and actually advocate certain issues in relation to women These are very important things that women can do; they've got to start coming out.

Sometimes, he stated, perceptions turn into reality, and that is what they as Afghans deeply involved in the reconstruction of their country were hoping for. Media can help reinforce positive messages and potentially encourage the creation of role models in society, which are truly in dire need in a country like Afghanistan.

Conclusion

The interview subjects featured in this chapter are all experts in their respective fields, and have either recently spent a considerable amount of time working in Afghanistan, or are still currently working in country. Without hesitation, these experts saw media as a critical component to the development of civil society, democracy, and women's rights and civic participation in the reconstruction of their country. Without a dynamic media, they stated that Afghanistan would be in a very different place right now, and the international community would not have gained the perception that there have been improvements within the country as well as the beginnings of a democratic system set in place. Media has acted as a powerful mirror, reflecting the positive and negative developments in country, helping to steer the country towards a more progressive direction by keeping it on the path of development and reconstruction.

The guiding central research question of "what role do media play in the midst of or in relationship to social change?" was invariably touched upon by each interview participant, and media was shown to be a key player in the emerging democracy of a post-conflict country such as Afghanistan. At the same time, media are facing unprecedented challenges at the time of writing of this thesis with new attempts by the government and conservative factions to curb freedom of expression and freedom of the press and enact more governmental control over this dynamic sector.

When Mr. Mohseni was asked whether he could ever foresee the complete shutdown of free media in Afghanistan, he responded:

> Can they shut the media down? Of course they can. No matter how much international presence there is, if the government decides that the free media is not useful to it, and wants to handle things in a more dictatorial manner, they can do it. Will it be good for Afghanistan? Absolutely not. It always starts with something like this. Dictatorships usually entail that the dictator thinks he knows what's right for the country. This is the start of a dictatorial regime. It can happen, and there's always a danger that it will happen. That's why there is an avid responsibility on the shoulders of the international community that this will not happen.

This suggests that the international community should not and cannot afford to abandon Afghanistan as it has repeatedly done in the past. Otherwise, this fragile democracy can easily slip back into a failed state existence where all of the strides made on behalf of the Afghan people will simply vanish, and human rights and freedom of the press will mean nothing at all. The opinions of these interview subjects underscore the importance of media in the midst of social change after so many years of chaos and oppressive rule. Media is the torchbearer of truth and public opinion, and after so many years of suppression of the Afghan people's voices, it is now time for them to be heard strong and clear without pause.

CHAPTER FIVE:

RESEARCH DESIGN AND METHODOLOGY

This chapter provides an overview of the research design and methodology used for the interview process, discusses documentary analysis used with secondary sources, and summarizes the particular methods and procedures adopted throughout the work which include qualitative interviewing and interpretive analysis. Biographies on each participant are provided (see Appendix III) to support the basis for why these interview subjects were chosen. The criteria used to make these choices are also discussed, along with a justification for the methods and approaches which were used to develop this empirically-focused (and partially theoretically-focused) work.

RESEARCH DESIGN:

The qualitative research techniques employed for this thesis consists of: (1) interviews and email exchanges with qualified experts in their field (based primarily on first-hand experience working in Afghanistan), including senior Afghan Government representatives, United Nations and humanitarian NGO (non-governmental organization) employees, human rights senior representatives, and media development experts; (2) a review and analysis of secondary sources, including United Nations studies, Afghan Government official documents, and reports done by leading institutions such as the World Bank and other NGOs; and, (3) critical examination of major concepts and theories from scholarly literature focused on theories of deliberative democracy.

METHODOLOGY:

Interview Data from Primary Sources

The interview subjects are all experts in their respective fields, and have had experience and exposure to the effects of emerging media, political and societal change, the electoral process, and reconstruction efforts in Afghanistan. Additionally, they have experience with gender issues in the country, and have worked to promote the legal, political and human rights of Afghan women. Information gathered from each area of expertise provides insight, broadens the scope of the study, and gives weight to the overall research argument and central research question by considering first-hand accounts and informed opinions of experienced professionals who have had significant exposure to the issues this work has investigated.

Blumler suggests that the researcher "seek participants in the sphere of life who are acute observers and who are well informed" (Blumler, 1969: 41). It is for this reason that experts in their field with first-hand experience working in Afghanistan were chosen to participate as interview subjects in this study, offering observations and well informed perspectives.

This study draws information from data collected via interviews and/or questionnaires. Interviews or questionnaires use a semi-structured format and a few open-ended questions to which the subjects were asked to respond. The questions posed were structured to elicit specific information about the role of media, empowerment of women, and the development of civil society, freedom of the press, and human rights in post-conflict Afghanistan. Additionally, the questions were designed to identify key factors and provide comparisons and contrasts with regard to the specific areas of interest mentioned above. Provisions were made allowing the interview subjects to provide any additional commentary they wished to make regarding the issues addressed in the questionnaire. The interview process is particularly useful when aspects of behavior or situations that are difficult to observe directly are collected through the interviews and/or questionnaires, enabling the assessment of attitudes and opinions on a variety of subjects, from political views to cultural practices.

Half of the interviews were conducted in person and half were conducted on the phone using a semi-structured questionnaire. Interviewees were selected on the basis of their level of experience and expertise in their respective fields, and exposure to key areas which emerged and were identified in the theoretically-focused analysis found in Chapter Two. Some of the interviewees are active in all of these key areas in post-conflict Afghanistan, and some were specifically focused on one or more area of expertise. Each interview lasted approximately 30 - 45 minutes. When deemed necessary, follow-up discussions with the interviewees were conducted through email exchange.

Once the interview subjects had indicated a willingness to participate in this study, they were electronically sent a list of semi-structured and open-ended questions through the use of email. During the actual interviews, there was room allowed to ask spontaneous questions of the interviewees, prompting more candid and open responses.

A total of 14 people were approached for interviews. However, four were not available and/or declined. A total of 10 interviews were conducted over an eight month period, starting in October 2005. The interview approach adopted was largely based on exploratory and standard interview techniques, which the author has professionally utilized during her five years experience as a television and print journalist.

The major limitation of the interview method is that it relies on a self-report method of data collection. Poor memory, misunderstandings and deception on the part of the subject can contribute to inaccuracies in the data collected. However, reporting on qualitative research involves careful description of what was heard, and how the subjects reacted and behaved. This may involve data summarization and categorization into themes or patterns, or it may involve description and interpretation of what was observed or heard during the interview process. The author's primary objective was to obtain qualitative data about the interview subjects' opinions and views on the role of media, empowerment of women, and issues surrounding the development of civil society, freedom of the press, and human rights in post-Taliban Afghanistan.

The data collected throughout the period of this study suggests that the views expressed by the interview subjects were relatively unbiased, and appear consistent with the opinions and views expressed by the other interview participants that were selected for this study. Each interview was transcribed in totality, and then quotes deemed critical and relevant to the study were extracted into a separate document. A sample questionnaire of the questions posed to the interview subjects may be found in Appendix II.

Criteria Selection for the Interview Subjects

The interview subjects were selected for this study on the basis of whether their fields of expertise and respective organizations dealt with or had any exposure to the role of media, empowerment of women, and the development of civil society, freedom of the press, and human rights in post-conflict Afghanistan. In all cases, the questionnaire was addressed to individuals in senior positions, who have all been published or covered in the media themselves for their respective roles in the reconstruction efforts of Afghanistan. Therefore, it is reasonable to conclude that the interviewees are well suited and credible subjects to provide information about the views and practices of their respective organizations, and share their valuable insight about the experiences and exposure they gained while working in Afghanistan. The interview subjects who participated were chosen based on their level of expertise, exposure to the issues, availability and willingness to participate in this study.

Documentary Analysis of Secondary Sources

In addition to the data obtained from the interview subjects, a number of materials and primary documents were drawn upon to illuminate the processes being examined in this book.   There is a growing body of United Nations studies, Afghan government documents, world institutions reports (World Bank, IMF, Asian Development Bank), non-governmental organization (NGO) reports, and academic papers offering supportive documentation and substantial discussion on the role of media and gender in post-conflict Afghanistan.   Documentary analysis was conducted to achieve a contextual understanding of relevant documents to the proposed study.

This study collected and analyzed data from these documents and reports to provide further support to the guiding central research question. Critical analysis and research has been conducted by the Afghan government, United Nations agencies, world institutions, and non-governmental organizations, which have had a focus and played a part in Afghanistan's renewal and reconstruction efforts. These documents provide insight to the working thesis, offering supportive evidence to the key themes which have been established in prior chapters, underpinning the transformation of post-conflict Afghanistan. Additionally, these supportive documents are not based in theory but in actual practice, stemming from organizations and individuals who are working "on the ground' in Afghanistan. Utilizing analysis and interpretation of these documents and reports yields key revelations to the benefit of the study.

Critical Examination of Scholarly Sources

Though this book is primarily an empirically-focused study, theoretical work was undertaken involving critical examination of major concepts and theories of deliberative democracy. Interpretative analysis was used to decipher the internal logic of arguments put forth by over 60 scholarly literature sources. The development of key themes related to the literature emerged from this analysis, and influenced the development of the research questions as well as the best way of organizing the book structure.

Intensive research was carried out to locate and investigate each scholarly source, exploring the relevance and appropriateness of inclusion in this particular study. Once deemed appropriate for research purposes, the relevant research literature was critically reviewed and selected materials and quotes were extracted into what rapidly became a 'large' and growing body of work. Obviously, it is not possible to cover all the literature available on the chosen topic; therefore, it was crucial that the author made critical selections carefully, highlighting key findings and arguments that help provide the justification and structure necessary for the study.

Once the key findings and quotations were organized into one main document, the selection of similar points of view and supportive materials needed to be gathered and arranged in an appropriate fashion. The development of the research questions posed to the interview subjects also emerged from the critical examination of these scholarly sources, aligning themselves with the key themes which emerged from the literature. In this manner, the interpretative work involved in the critical examination of major concepts and theories of deliberative democracy paved the way for the creation of the entire study, helping to shape each resulting chapter included in this book.

CHAPTER SIX:

CONCLUSION: A LONG ROAD AHEAD FOR AFGHANISTAN

As illustrated in previous discussions on deliberative democracy in Chapters Two and Four, there is no doubt that media play a critical and instrumental role in all of modern day societies. Post-conflict Afghanistan is no exception. Radio, print, and television have been active media throughout Afghanistan's more recent history. Now the presence of satellite television and the Internet are growing in popularity as new technologies make their way into the urban centers of the country. The rural areas are still quite limited in access to various media, with radio remaining the dominant source of information due to high levels of illiteracy and limited electricity (Rawan, 2002; World Press Encyclopedia, 2003).

The Afghan media have done much to call attention to injustices and inequities throughout society, taking on the "watchdog" role described by Norris (2000); however, serious challenges remain facing the fledgling media in this war-torn nation.

"As a country entrenched in the beginning stages of progress, in fact, Afghanistan has substantial barriers to media development. These obstacles include inhospitable terrain, mixed ethnic groups with historic conflicts, language differences, low literacy and income levels, undeveloped educational and other social welfare institutions, and a governmental structure dominated by religious intolerance" (World Press Encyclopedia, 2003, p. 2). Although this quotation is from 2003, it remains relevant three years later. The media in Afghanistan are a dynamic force, pushing the envelope within society, forcing the powers that be to reckon with injustices and hypocrisy, taking risks that have resulted in death and injury, and upholding tenets of democracy such as civil society, freedom of the press, and human rights under situations of duress and pressure of censorship. Theories of deliberative democracy point to these same facets of media as requirements that any

83

good democratic society should uphold and encourage to nurture a healthy media presence.

According to Saad Mohseni, the Director of Tolo TV and Arman FM Radio in Kabul, media are the strongest and most promising sector to have developed so far in post-Taliban Afghanistan:

> Of the Three Pillars, the Executive Branch is a failure, the Parliamentary and Legislative Branch may be vocal but it's ineffective, it really hasn't done anything, and the Judicial Branch is in total disarray. The Fourth Pillar is, of course, media. Media have been a shining example of what Afghanistan has achieved which has been the envy of the region, of the Muslim world.

Indeed, the future success of Afghanistan as a country will undoubtedly be linked to upholding tenets of democracy, freedom of the press, and respect for human rights, otherwise it will remain in danger of repeating its tragic history once again. This is why it is crucial for the international community to stay patient and stay committed to the reconstruction and social renewal of this war-ravaged country, otherwise face the inevitable consequences of increased terrorism and failed state status yet again.

The empowerment of women is a concept that is very difficult to predict or measure at this critical juncture in the transition to democracy in post-Taliban Afghanistan. However, the majority of signs indicate that Afghan women are still some of the most oppressed in the world. There have definitely been some bold strides within media and politics to include and encourage women's participation, but this does not adequately reflect the lives of the mass majority of Afghan women who still suffer the highest maternal mortality rate in the world, epidemic levels of illiteracy and unemployment, and continuous human rights violations including domestic violence, under-age marriage and rape (United Nations Development Fund for Women (UNIFEM), 2004).

84

Theories of deliberative democracy illustrate that for a polity to reflect a healthy representation of itself within the scope of society, it requires full and equal participation of its entire citizenry, which includes both men and women. The active participation of Afghan women in media and politics appears to be helping to erode the age-old gender imbalance in Afghanistan that has largely prevented women's access to society. As was previously discussed by several interviewees, role models have emerged in the media and political spheres providing examples of active women participating in society for both men and women to absorb and hopefully accept. Radio, and more recently television, has contributed to the advent of stronger roles for women in Afghan society, and even the emergence of some feminist thinking in Islamic societies. However, there is a very long way to go until Afghan society exhibits full support and respect for women's rights and civic participation, as expressed by all of the interview subjects in this thesis. The empowerment of women will not be so easily addressed or attained in the specific case of post-conflict Afghanistan.

Given the dire human index indicators and statistics, it is important to recognize that development in Afghan society in all sectors and on all levels cannot move forward if the legal framework does not support equality in the law for all of Afghanistan's citizens. "Ensuring that Afghan women can participate equally in the political life in Afghanistan, have equal opportunities for education and employment, equal access to health care, and other rights, must not only emanate from the laws and legal institutions through a "top down" approach, but also through social and development programs through a "bottom up" approach" (Nawabi, 2003, p. 7). This approach should assist in the greater attainment of rights for Afghan women, and help realize the benefits of such strides throughout the socioeconomic and political life of the nation. Without true equality and public participation in all aspects of society, Afghan women will continue to suffer and remain some of the most oppressed of their kind the worldwide over.

Previous chapters have reflected upon the significance of media in a democratic society, reviewed the media's role towards women's empowerment, civic participation and human rights, and attempted to contextualize the argument within the Afghan context. Another major debate that relates to how democratic tradition itself has addressed the question of gender has not been delved into in great depth in this particular study. It has been shown that freedom of the press, the expectations associated with it, and the perception of media as a part of the public sphere are closely linked with democratic principles. In fact, the conception of democratic media is a creation of democratic tradition. However, in a post-conflict nation such as Afghanistan, one has to question the relevance of the public sphere and whether it can or does actually exist in such an environment.

The discussion in Chapter Two makes some reference to the gendered nature of democratic theory. However, there may not be a direct connection between the gendered nature of democracy and the absence of women's issues on the media's agenda. The underlying argument pertains to the marginalization of women's concerns both in the public sphere of media and democracy. Theories of deliberative democracy draw largely from Western thought and literature since the democratic model of governance originally developed in the West. How relevant and applicable these theories are to an Eastern and Islamic culture is in question, where cultural, economic, social and religious values seem to be so contrasting to those found in the West, contributing to many misunderstandings between the Christian-Judeo and Islamic worlds. Most of these theories and ideologies have little relevance in a post-conflict country such as Afghanistan, still grappling to steady itself after nearly a quarter century of war and social upheaval. As previously mentioned in a recent UNDP study, Afghanistan ranks as the fifth poorest country in the world with some of the worst human indicators on the planet (United Nations Development Programme (UNDP) & Islamic Republic of Afghanistan, 2004).

A huge gap exists between theory and practice as far as women's rights and status are concerned in Afghanistan. Media seem to have fared much better though not without its current and ongoing challenges. Though there are bright signs and positive indicators to celebrate in this post-Taliban period, women's subordination has become a naturalized way of life in Afghanistan's patriarchal social context, and largely remains unquestioned at both the societal and state levels.

However, for a public sphere to exist in any semblance requires true equality and equity among all its citizens, not just its male constituency, in order to reflect a balanced polity where communicative action and civic participation can freely occur. This viewpoint is expressed from Habermas to Calhoun to Benhabib and beyond among theorists of deliberative democracy. Consequently, an informed citizenry is essential to the functioning of democratic regimes, where knowledge is regarded as a critical element of democratic citizenship, "as more informed citizens have civic attributes that characterize the qualities of good citizenship" (McGraw, 2003, p.400). Better-informed citizens express more support for democratic norms and values such as tolerance and civil liberties, and are more likely to participate in politics through voting and elections. Though the Afghan Parliament reflects nearly 26 percent of its participants as women, which is an exciting, new development considering the country's recent past, this is only scratching at the surface at what seemingly appears to be an insurmountable mass of problems still plaguing this post-conflict country.

When asked whether democracy will ever take hold in a country like Afghanistan, all of the interview subjects responded positively but not without reservation and great concern about the future course of Afghanistan if the following areas did not see vast improvement: 1) peace and security; 2) rule of law and governance; 3) education; and, 4) respect for women's and human rights. There are many other problems and concerns to be addressed in this war-torn nation. However, these four areas seemed to top the list for the interviewees. There are concerns that if these areas are not tackled by both the Afghan Government and international community in the most proactive and hands-on manner, democratic progress will be stalled and only a superficial foundation will exist, leaving itself vulnerable to both ideological and terrorist attacks, and a reversal in societal development.

A healthy functioning democracy is a system of government in which ultimate political authority is vested in the people. Although this may only exist as an ideal, the starting presupposition is that citizens are sufficiently informed about political and social matters that they are able to reach sound judgments and decisions. Thus, reliable and unbiased information is vital to the health of the democratic state; information is the catalyst that allows democracies to function, and the media are the principle mechanism through which information is disseminated and learned. Consequently, the media play a central role in contemporary democracies. Therefore, it is crucial that media be allowed to flourish and grow in post-conflict Afghanistan in order to ensure that civil society can develop and support women's and human rights, freedom of the press and freedom of expression, and that the Afghan people are made aware and educated about the circumstances they have endured and continue to face in this historic transformation to democracy in post-Taliban Afghanistan.

Afghanistan will only become a true democracy when citizens can turn for help to locally elected leaders, rather than armed warlords. That is why the electoral process is so important, and that is why freedom of the press is essential in assisting the development of democracy in a country that is historically unfamiliar with and challenged by the concepts of equality and equity for all of its citizens. The role of media is crucial in the development of human rights and civil society in this post-conflict country, just as it is integral in the empowerment of Afghan women in politics and society. The two are intrinsically linked.

Today the voices of these women must be heard because they represent hope for Afghanistan to become a legitimate, sovereign nation that respects the equality and rights of its citizens through a democratic constitution. Their example must be held up to others who live in fear that they have no voice.

The role of the media, empowerment of women, and the development of civil society, freedom of the press, and human rights in post-Taliban Afghanistan have not been a focus of many studies. The topic of emerging media in Afghanistan is a dynamic and important one that needs to be thoroughly explored and investigated. The changing role of Afghan women in politics and society is yet another new phenomenon to be studied. If any future research is carried out in this particular area of study, it is recommended that it build upon the work done here, adding to the interpretive analysis and qualitative interviewing process that has been undertaken in this empirically-grounded work.

These evolving aspects of life in Afghanistan are a reflection of the metamorphoses the Afghan society and people themselves are experiencing, and they contain the raw expressions and unpredictable nature of such epochal change. This is a historic time in the transformation of Afghanistan, marked by challenge, excitement and sometimes violence as this country struggles to find its new voice and identity in the twenty-first century.

APPENDIX I

CHRONOLOGY OF POLITICAL EVENTS

1747 Country officially named and recognized as Afghanistan.

1880-1901 Amir Abdur Rahman. Attempt to abolish levirate, raise the marriageable age, and grant women divorce rights under specific circumstances.

1901-1919 Amir Habibullah. Creates a ceiling for marriage expenses. Killed in 1919.

1919 Third Anglo-Afghan War whereby Afghanistan regained full independence.

1919-29 King Amanullah. Afghanistan's first Constitution and legal reforms introduced. Attempt to modernize society and culture. Marriageable age for women raised to 18 years and for men 21 years. Polygamy abolished.

1929 King Amanullah exiled as a result of tribal uprising against reform policy. Civil War.

1930-33 King Nadir Shah. Installed with support of tribes and religious establishment. Assassinated in 1933.

1933-73 Zahir Shah reigns.

1949 Election reforms result in liberal parliament. Marriage Law passed. Purdah is made optional; women enter University, workforce and government.

1950 Crackdown on nascent opposition and end of liberal experiment. Sardar Daoud becomes Prime Minister in 1953. Rapprochement with the Soviet Union.

1963 Daoud forced to resign, mainly because of authoritarian style of government and strained relations with Pakistan. Constitution and first nationwide election.

1963-73 Constitutional monarchy and parliamentary democracy installed. Failed due to lack of enactment of the Constitution and not legalizing political parties. Formation of Communist and of Islamist groupings, which increasingly clash at the university campus.

1971-73 Severe droughts resulting in famine mainly in Central Afghanistan. Government perceived as inactive and unable to manage the crisis.

1973 Coup d'etat by Sardar Daoud assisted by Communist group Parcham. Reform policy started, and restrictions on political opponents.

1975 Attempts of Islamic insurgency failed. Clamp down on Islamic opponents.

1977 New Constitution. Civil Code and Penal Code (based on Shari'a but no *hadd* punishments). Women get equal rights to institute divorce cases. Family Courts established. Clamp down on communist opponents.

1978 Saur Revolution: Bloody coup against President Daoud by united communist groups Khalq/Parcham (PDPA). Nur Mohammad Taraki as Prime Minister. 1977 Constitution abrogated. Decree No. 7 confirms equal rights for women, regularizes dowry and marriage expenses and forbids forced marriages. Decree No. 8 introduces comprehensive but ill-founded land reform.

1979 Widespread popular insurgency, followed by brutal suppression. Infighting in the PDPA and Taraki killed and replaced by Hafizullah Amin. In December, 50,000 Soviet troops invade the country. Hafizullah Amin is killed, and Barbrak Karmal installed as President.

1989 Withdrawal of Soviet troops. Mujahuddin control most of countryside, increasing number of refugees escape fighting and destruction. Over the next decade, the number of refugees reaches around six million.

1992 President Najibullah agrees to step down and mujahuddin coalition takes over Kabul. In-fighting over the next couple of years leads to the destruction of Kabul and Kandahar. Decree on *hijab* issued restricts women's public appearance.

1994 Emergence of Taliban.

1996 Taliban conquer Kabul, Najibullah executed. Ban on women's employment, girls' schools closed, full purdah imposed on women and ban on men shaving their beards.

1998 Taliban conquer Mazar-i-Sharif, the last major city controlled by Northern Alliance.

1999 The UN imposes sanctions against Afghanistan. Drought hits the country.

2001 Third year of drought. Taliban regime falls. Signing of Bonn Agreement. Hamid Karzai chosen leader of Interim Government.

2002 Emergency Loya Jirga convenes in Kabul. Transitional Government assigned.

2004 New Constitution agreed by Loya Jirga.

2004 First Democratic Presidential Election.

2005 Parliamentary and Provincial Council Elections

2009 Second Democratic Presidential Election

(Adapted from previous World Bank and United Nations reports)

APPENDIX II

SAMPLE QUESTIONNAIRE

AFGHAN WOMEN, MEDIA AND DEMOCRACY:
Emerging Democracy in Post-Taliban Afghanistan

Questions for Khorshied Samad, M.A. Thesis, Department of Communication, University of Ottawa, Canada:

#1: What role do media play in Afghan society?

#2: How do media facilitate the transition to democracy and development of civil society in post-Taliban Afghanistan, if at all?

#3: Do media empower Afghan women in politics and/or society? How so if yes or no?

#4: What role do Afghan women play in the reconstruction of their country, if at all?

#5: What further developments need to occur to foster the transition to democracy in post-Taliban Afghanistan?

#6: Any closing remarks?

Please answer these questions, and return via email to: Khorshied@gmail.com, or we will schedule an interview in person or over the telephone.

Many thanks!!

Khorshied Samad

APPENDIX III

SHORT BIOGRAPHIES OF INTERVIEW SUBJECTS

The author has chosen to include these short biographies to illustrate the level of experience and expertise that each of the interview subjects possesses, underscoring why these particular subjects were chosen to participate in this study.

1. His Excellency Ambassador Omar Samad; Afghan Ambassador to Canada. Interview: 10/11/05 (in person).

Short Biography: H.E. Ambassador Omar Samad is a notable authority on the history and contributing factors of media development in Afghanistan, as well as a participant in its media history – as a journalist, activist, spokesperson, and now in the role of ambassador. Ambassador Omar Samad has represented Afghanistan for nearly 25 years, since he was forced to flee his country soon after the Soviet Invasion in 1979, and as a young student organized the first Afghan Students Association in the United States. After the tragedies of 9/11 and the fall of the Taliban, he became a top news commentator for a host of US television networks, before becoming the special Bonn Correspondent for CNN, covering the Bonn Accords in December 2001. At the end of 2001, Ambassador Samad returned to live and work in Afghanistan, after a 22-year absence from his country, becoming the Spokesperson for the Foreign Ministry of Afghanistan and the Director General of Communication for the Transitional State of Afghanistan from 2001 – 2004. As part of the official Afghan delegation with President Karzai and Foreign Minister Dr. A. Abdullah, he attended high-level diplomatic meetings, international donor conferences, UN General Assemblies, World Economic Forums, and bilateral talks on the recovery and post-conflict reconstruction of Afghanistan with the leaders of the world. Ambassador Samad left Afghanistan for his position as Afghan Ambassador to

Canada in September 2004, where he currently resides and works in the capital city of Ottawa.

2. Ms. Clementina Cantoni, former Project Director of HAWA (Helping Afghan Widows Assistance) program for CARE International, Kabul, Afghanistan.

Interview: 10/29/05 (in person).

Short Biography: Ms. Cantoni, an international aid worked, lived and worked in Afghanistan from March 2002 until June 2005, helping to promote and improve the lives of Afghan women in society. Whether through improving access to healthcare and clinics in remote villages when she worked for IMC (International Medical Corps), or through developing a successful work program that trained and helped place widows in the labor market when she worked for CARE International, Ms. Cantoni devoted her energies to improving the lives of thousands of Afghan women. It was this dedication that inspired several thousand Afghan widows and women to take to the streets of Kabul in protest when Ms. Cantoni was kidnapped and held hostage by a group of armed criminals. She was thankfully released unharmed after 26 days of captivity. Ms. Cantoni is currently the Assistant Country Director for CARE International in Nairobi.

3. Mr. Peter Erben, former Director of the JEMB (Joint Electoral Management Body), Kabul, Afghanistan. Interview: 01/31/06 (on the phone from Jerusalem).

Short Biography: Peter Erben is a Senior Advisor with IFES and the Deputy Director of the Center for Transitional and Post-Conflict Governance. From this platform he specializes in the management of electoral projects in emerging democracies and is continuously engaged in key positions in major electoral processes. Since 2002, Mr. Erben has remained engaged as the Senior Expert for the

95

elections in the Palestinian territory. In 2005, Mr. Erben was seconded to the United Nations as the Chief Electoral Officer of Afghanistan, in charge of conducting the 2005 parliamentary and provincial council elections - a project engaging more than 180,000 staff at its peak with a budget of $165 million. In 2004 and 2005, Peter Erben was engaged by the International Organization for Migration (IOM) as the Director of the two Out-of-Country-Voting programs for the October 2004 Afghan Presidential election and for the January 2005 Iraqi National Assembly Elections. In 2002, Mr. Erben coordinated the EU Observation Mission to the Presidential Elections in East Timor and thereafter acted as the Senior Election Advisor to the Afghan Emergency Loya Jirga (Grand Council) Commission in Kabul. In this capacity he organized the final stage of the first presidential election following the war in Afghanistan.

4. Jane McElhone; former Project Director for IMPACS (Institute for Media, Policy and Civil Society), Kabul, Afghanistan. Interview: 02/10/06 (in person).

Short Biography: Ms. McElhone is a journalist by training; however, over the last few years she worked in various countries to develop press freedom, focusing on journalism training and media development. She lived and worked in Afghanistan from January 2003 until August 2005, first as a journalism trainer specifically working to train Afghan women in the media, and then running a project funded by the Canadian International Development Agency (CIDA) that worked to train Afghan women in the media, create employment for women in the media, and give a voice to women in the media so that women's issues would be discussed by women, talking about their own issues. IMPACS is a Canadian NGO based in Vancouver. Ms. McElhone now resides in London, where she is the Media Development Coordinator for OSI (the Open Society Institute), an international NGO.

5. Dr. Sima Samar, Chairperson of the Afghanistan Independent Human Rights Commission. Former Minister of Women's Affairs, and Vice-Chair to President Karzai, Kabul, Afghanistan. Interview: 02/13/06 (in person).

Short Biography: Dr. Sima Samar is a well known woman's and human rights advocate and activist within national and international forums. Since 1994, Dr. Samar has received various international awards on women's rights, human rights, democracy, and women for peace, including the Kennedy Center's Profile in Courage Award and the John Humphrey Award in Canada. Dr. Samar served as the first Deputy Chair and Minister of Women's Affairs in the Interim Administration of Afghanistan in 2002. Before chairing the Commission, she was elected as the Vice Chair of the Emergency Loya Jirga. She was appointed as the Chair of the AIHRC by President Karzai, President of the Islamic Republic of Afghanistan.

6. Mr. Grant Kippen. Former Country Director for NDI (National Democratic Institute), and former Chair of Electoral Complaints Commission, Kabul, Afghanistan. Interview: 03/07/06 (in person).

Short Biography: Mr. Kippen worked from 2003 – 2004 in Kabul, Afghanistan as the Country Director for NDI, a Washington, DC-based NGO, and from May through October 2005 as the Chair of the Electoral Complaints Commission appointed jointly by the UN and the Afghan Government, the first independent electoral complaints commission established in Afghanistan's history, amended to the electoral law of Afghanistan. The commission investigated and adjudicated over 7,000 complaints during the parliamentary elections. During the first democratic Presidential Elections held in October 2004, a number of complaints arose about the elections themselves, and the EU and other international observation groups as well as domestic groups suggested that an independent electoral complaints commission should be formed, with the intention of satisfying people's doubts and inquiries during the electoral process through transparency and professional conduct. Two out of five of the electoral complaints commissioners were women, with the five members being assigned by the UN, Afghan Supreme Court and Afghanistan Independent Human Rights Commission. Mr. Kippen resides in Ottawa, but is currently working on a UN project in Bangladesh.

7. Zohra Rasekh, Director of the Office of Human Rights and International Women's Affairs, Ministry of Foreign Affairs, Kabul, Afghanistan. Interview: 03/25/06 (on the phone from Washington, DC).

Short Biography: The Office of Human Rights and International Women's Affairs is a fairly new office, established in 2003, and deals with international conventions related to human rights; and acts as a liaison or coordinating body with the international community and Afghanistan Government in relation to women's issues. All international partners coordinate through the office, and the office is also in charge of mobilizing resources in the areas of gender and women's issues, helping with formulating policies in terms of women's situations in Afghanistan. Afghanistan has signed 6 international human rights treaties, including CEDAW (Convention on Elimination of all forms of Discrimination against Women). The office is in the process of training 15 key line ministries as well as government officials in understanding the human rights treaties that have been ratified by Afghanistan, to have the knowledge and ability to recognize the conventions, and be able to properly report them to the UN and implement them. Implementation of these human rights treaties are part of the Afghanistan Compact strategy and UN Millennium Goals.

8. Ms. Rina Amiri, former Political Officer, UNAMA, Kabul, Afghanistan. Interview: 04/23/06 (on the phone from New York City).

Short Biography: Ms. Amiri worked in Afghanistan from March 2002 until February 2006 as the Political Officer and Special Advisor to the SRSG (Special Representative for the Secretary General) for UNAMA (The United Nations Assistance Mission to Afghanistan). Her role was working in the main office of the SRSG, and advising on the implementation of the Bonn Agreement, which was recently completed with the final benchmark of achieving Parliamentary and Provincial Council Elections. She also was in charge of helping organize voter registration for Afghan women, Kuchis, IDPs (Internally Displaced People), Hindus and Sikhs for both the Presidential Elections of 2004 and the Parliamentary Elections of 2005. Ms. Amiri now works and resides in New York City.

9. Roya Rahmani, Project Coordinator, Women's Rights in Afghanistan Fund, Rights and Democracy, Kabul, Afghanistan. Interview: 05/20/06 (on the phone from Montreal, Canada).

Short Biography: Ms. Rahmani runs the Kabul office for Rights and Democracy, a Canadian NGO. The official name for the NGO is International Center for Human Rights and Democratic Development. One of their largest projects is located in Kabul, which was established in 2003. This human rights organization has a mandate focused on globalization, democratic development, women's rights, and aboriginal rights. The project she heads is called Women's Rights in Afghanistan Fund, funded 100% by CIDA, focusing on supporting women's organizations in Afghanistan with grants, helping them design and implement their projects in a better way. R&D is also helping to develop programs which assist with capacity-building, especially among Afghan women leaders, and they are developing projects which involve lobbying and advocacy work.

10. Mr. Saad Mohseni, Executive Director of TOLO TV and ARMAN FM RADIO, Kabul, Afghanistan. Interview: 06/23/06 (on the phone from Kabul, Afghanistan).

Short Biography: Saad Mohseni is the Founder and Executive Director of both Tolo TV and Arman FM Radio stations located in Kabul, Afghanistan. Tolo TV was launched in October 2004, becoming one of the first commercial television stations to operate in Afghanistan, and laying the foundations for an accessible media outlet offering local and international news, sports, current affairs, movies, comedy, serials, documentaries, music, children's programming, lifestyle and entertainment shows. Arman FM Radio, the first commercial radio station in Afghanistan, launched in April 2003, and now has 11 Million listeners through the use of satellite radio transmitters in five major urban centers throughout the country. After years of war, oppression and destruction, the Afghans are ready to move on. Tolo TV and Arman FM Radio aim to assist this effort by providing content which will educate, inform, entertain and inspire all Afghans. Mr. Mohseni is an Australian-Afghan, who returned to live and work in his birth country in 2002.

BIBLIOGRAPHY

Abirafeh, L. (2005). *Lessons from Gender-focused International Aid in Post-Conflict Afghanistan...Learned?* Munich: Freidrich Ebert Stiftung.

Afghanistan Independent Human Rights Committee (AIHRC). (2006). Afghan Women's Rights Report [Electronic Version], . Retrieved February 14, 2006 from www.aihrc.org.

Anwar, R. (1988). *The Tragedy of Afghanistan: A First-hand Account.* London: Verso.

Aristotle. (1986). *Aristotle's Politics* (Apostle, Hippocrates & L. Gerson, Trans.). Grinnell, Iowa: The Peripatetic Press.

Article 19, & Global Campaign for Free Expression. (2006). *Memorandum on Afghan Mass Media Law.* London: Article 19.

Barber, B. (1998). *A Place for Us: How to Make Society Civil and Democracy Strong.* New York: Hill and Wang.

Barnett, C. (2003). *Culture and Democracy: Media, Space, and Representation.* Tuscaloosa: The University of Alabama Press.

Bathla, S. (1998). *Women, Democracy and the Media: Cultural and Political Representation in the Indian Press.* New Delhi: Sage Publications India Private, Ltd.

Benhabib, S. (1996). Toward a Deliberative Model of Democratic Legitimacy. In S. Benhabib (Ed.), *Democracy and Difference: Contesting the boundaries of the political* (pp. 67-95). Princeton: Princeton University Press.

Blumler, J. G. (1969). *Television in Politics: Its Uses and Influences.* Chicago: University of Chicago Press.

Calhoun, C. (Ed.). (1992). *Habermas and the Public Sphere.* Cambridge: MIT Press.

Calsamiglia, A. (1999). Constitutionalism and Democracy. In H. Hongju Koh & R. Slye (Eds.), *Deliberative Democracy and Human Rights* (pp. 136-143). New Haven: Yale University Press.

Cohen, J. (1996). Procedure and Substance in Deliberative Democracy. In S. Benhabib (Ed.), *Democracy and Difference: Contesting the boundaries of the political* (pp. 95-120). Princeton: Princeton University Press.

Cohen, J. L. (1996). Democracy, Difference and the Right of Privacy. In S. Benhabib (Ed.), *Democracy and Difference: Contesting the boundaries of the political* (pp. 187-218). Princeton: Princeton University Press.

Coleman, I., & Hunt, S. (2006, April 24). Afghanistan should make room for its female leaders. *Christian Science Monitor.*

Cunningham, F. (2002). *Theories of Democracy: A critical introduction.* London: Routledge.

Dahl, R. (1971). *Polyarchy: Participation and Opposition.* New Haven: Yale University Press.

Dahlgren, P. (1991). *Communication and Citizenship: Journalism and the Public Sphere in the Media Age.* London: Routledge.

Dahlgren, P. (2000). The Internet and the Democratization of Civic Culture. *Political Communication, 17*(4), 335-340.

Dahlgren, P. (2001). The Transformation of Democracy? In B. Axford & R. Huggins (Eds.), *New Media and Politics* (pp. 64-89). London: Sage Publications.

De Montesquieu, B. (1914). *The Spirit of Laws* (T. Nugent, Trans.). London: G. Bell & Sons, Ltd.

Dryzek, J. (2000). *Deliberative Democracy and Beyond: Liberals, Critics, Contestations.* Oxford: Oxford University Press.

Dupree, N. H. (1977). *Afghanistan: An Historical Guide to Afghanistan.* Kabul: Kabul Air Authority, Kabul Tourism Organization.

Eickelman, D. F., & Anderson, J. W. (1999). *New Media in the Muslim World: The Emerging Public Sphere.* Bloomington: Indiana University Press.

Esfandiari, G. (2006). Afghanistan: Afghan Women Journalists Fight Restrictions, Threats. Prague: Radio Free Europe/Radio Liberty.

Farivar, M. (1999). *Dateline Afghanistan: Journalism under the Taliban*. New York: Committee to Protect Journalists.

Fraser, N. (1992). Rethinking the Public Sphere: A contribution to the critique of actually existing democracy. In C. Calhoun (Ed.), *Habermas and the Public Sphere* (pp. 100-121). Cambridge: MIT Press.

Goodin, R. (2003). Democratic Deliberation Within. In J. Fishkin & P. Laslett (Eds.), *Debating Deliberative Democracy* (pp. 54-79). Malden: Blackwell Publishing.

Goodson, L. (2001). *Afghanistan's Endless War*. Seattle: University of Washington Press.

Gould, C. C. (1996). Diversity and Democracy: Representing Difference. In S. Benhabib (Ed.), *Democracy and Difference: Contesting the Boundaries of the Political* (pp. 171-187). Princeton: Princeton University Press.

Government of Afghanistan. (1964). *Constitution of Afghanistan*. Kabul: Government of Afghanistan.

Government of Afghanistan. (2002). *National Development Framework*. Kabul: Government of Afghanistan, UNAMA.

Government of Afghanistan. (2004). *Constitution of Afghanistan*. Kabul: Government of Afghanistan.

Gurevitch, M., & Blumler, J. G. (1995). *The Crisis of Public Communication*. London: Routledge.

Gutmann, A. (1996). Democracy, Philosophy, and Justification. In S. Benhabib (Ed.), *Democracy and Difference: Contesting the boundaries of the political* (pp. 340-347). Princeton: Princeton University Press.

Habermas, J. (1989). *The Structural Transformation of the Public Sphere: An Inquiry into a Category of Bourgeois Society* (T. Burger, Trans.). Cambridge: MIT Press.

Habermas, J. (1991). The Public Sphere. In C. Mukerji & M. Schudson (Eds.), *Rethinking Popular Culture: Contemporary perspectives in cultural studies* (pp. 398-404). Berkeley: University of California Press.

Habermas, J. (1996). *Between Facts and Norms: Contributions to a Discourse Theory of Law and Democracy*. Cambridge: MIT Press.

Hans, A. (2004). Escaping Conflict: Afghan Women in Transit. In W. Giles & J. Hyndman (Eds.), *Sites of Violence: Gender and Conflict Zones* (pp. 103-136). Berkeley: University of California Press.

Huntington, S. (1991a). Democracy's Third Wave. *Journal of Democracy, 13*(2), 3-13.

Huntington, S. (1991b). *The Third Wave: Democratization in the Late Twentieth Century*. Norman: University of Oklahoma Press.

Hyman, A. (1992). *Afghanistan under Soviet Domination, 1964-91* (3rd ed.): St. Martin's Press.

Ibrahimi, S. (2006). The Limits of Press Freedom. *International War and Peace Reporting (IWPR)*.

Integrated Regional Information Networks (IRIN). (2006). Afghanistan: Year in Review 2005 - Fragile progress, insecurity remains. Retrieved January 28, 2006, from www.irinnews.org

Kandiyoti, D. (2005). *The Politics of Gender and Reconstruction in Afghanistan*. Geneva: United Nations Research Institute for Social Development.

Kant, I. (1947). *Perpetual Peace: A Philosophical Sketch*. La Salle: Open Court Publishing Company.

Katz, E. (1998). Mass Media and Participatory Democracy. In T. Inoguchi, E. Newman & J. Keane (Eds.), *The Changing Nature of Democracy* (pp. 87-100). Tokyo: United Nations University Press.

Keane, J. (1995). Structural Transformation of the Public Sphere? *Communication Review, 1*, 1-22.

Lacey, K. (1996). *Feminine Frequencies: Gender, German Radio, and the Public Sphere, 1923 - 1945*. Ann Arbor: University of Michigan Press.

Landes, J. B. (1996). The Performance of Citizenship: Democracy, Gender, and Difference in the French Revolution. In S. Benhabib (Ed.), *Democracy and Difference: Contesting the boundaries of the political* (pp. 295-313). Princeton: Princeton University Press.

Locke, J. (1970). *Two Treatises of Government*. Cambridge: Cambridge University Press.

Manin, B. (1997). *The Principles of Representative Government*. Cambridge: Cambridge University Press.

Mansbridge, J. (1999). Using Power/Fighting Power: The Polity. In H. Hongju Koh & R. Slye (Eds.), *Deliberative Democracy and Human Rights* (pp. 46-67). New Haven: Yale University Press.

Marsden, P. (1998). *The Taliban: War, Religion, and the New Order in Afghanistan*. London: Zed.

McGraw, K., & Holbrook, A. (2003). Democracy and the Media. In *Encyclopedia of International Media and Communications* (Vol. 1, pp. 399-408). Michigan: Elsevier Science.

Mill, J. S. (1991). *Considerations on Representative Government*. Oxford: Oxford University Press.

Nawabi, M. (2003). *Women's Rights in the New Constitution of Afghanistan*. Washington, D.C.: Georgetown University Law Center.

Norris, P. (2000). *A Virtuous Circle: Political communications in postindustrial societies*. New York: Cambridge University Press.

Parekh, B. (1993). The Cultural Particularity of Liberal Democracy. In D. Held (Ed.), *Prospects for Democracy* (pp. 160-172). Cambridge: Polity Press.

Pateman, C. (1988). *The Sexual Contract*. Stanford: Stanford University Press.

Phillips, A. (1996). Dealing with Difference: A politics of ideas, or a politics of presence? In S. Benhabib (Ed.), *Democracy and Difference: Contesting the boundaries of the political* (pp. 139-153). Princeton: Princeton University Press.

Putnam, R. (2000). *Bowling Alone: The collapse and rival of American community*. New York: Simon & Schuster.

Rashid, A. (2000). *Taliban: Islam, Oil, and Fundamentalism in Central Asia*. London: I.B. Tauris.

Rawan, S. M. (2002). Modern Mass Media and Traditional Communication in Afghanistan. *Political Communication, 19*, 155-170.

Razi, M. (1994). Afghanistan. In Y. Kamalipour & H. Mowlana (Eds.), *Mass Media in the Middle East: A Comprehensive Handbook*. Westport: Greenwood Press.

Reporters Sans Frontiers. (2006). Members of Parliament beat cameraman; journalists threatened by provincial council. *Reporters Sans Frontiers*.

Rivers, C. (2006). Where have all the women gone? [Electronic Version]. *Women's eNews*. Retrieved May 24, 2006 from http://www.alternet.org/mediaculture/15677/.

Rousseau, J.-J. (1968). *The Social Contract*. London: Penguin Books Ltd.

Sakr, N. (2004a). Women-Media Interaction in the Middle East: An introductory overview. In N. Sakr (Ed.), *Women and Media in the Middle East: Power through self-expression* (pp. 1-14). London: I.B. Tauris and Co., Ltd.

Sakr, N. (Ed.). (2004b). *Women and Media in the Middle East: Power through self-expression*. London: I.B. Tauris and Co. Ltd.

Sassi, S. (2001). The Transformation of the Public Sphere? In B. Axford & R. Huggins (Eds.), *New Media and Politics* (pp. 89-109). London: Sage Publications.

Schlesinger, P., & Tumber, H. (1995). *Reporting Crime: The Media Politics of Criminal Justice*. Oxford: Oxford University Press.

Schudson, M. (1992). Was there ever a Public Sphere? If so, when? Reflections on the American case. In C. Calhoun (Ed.), *Habermas and the Public Sphere*. (pp. 143-163). Cambridge: MIT Press.

Schudson, M. (1995). *The Power of News*. Cambridge: Harvard University Press.

Schudson, M. (2000). The Sociology of News Production Revisited (Again). In J. Curran & M. Gurevitch (Eds.), *Mass Media and Society* (pp. 175-200). London: Hodder Arnold H&S.

Sedra, M., & Middlebrook, P. (2004). *Afghanistan's problematic path to peace: Lessons in state-building in the post-September 11 era.* Toronto: Foreign Policy in Focus (FPIF).

Sen, A. (1999). *Development as Freedom.* Oxford: Oxford University Press.

Sunstein, C. (2003). The Law of Group Polarization. In J. Fishkin & P. Laslett (Eds.), *Debating Deliberative Democracy* (pp. 80-101). Malden: Blackwell Publishing.

Taras, D. (2001). Fragmentation Bombs: the New Media and the Erosion of Public Life. In *Power and Betrayal in the Canadian Media.* Peterborough: Broadview Press.

Tarzi, A. (2006). Afghanistan: The Brief History of Media Freedom. Prague: Radio Free Europe/Radio Liberty.

The Europa World Book. (2005). Afghanistan. In *The Europa World Book 2005* (Vol. 1, pp. 441-445). London: Routledge.

The World Bank. (2004). *Afghanistan: State Building, Sustaining Growth, and Reducing Poverty.* Washington, D.C.: The World Bank.

The World Bank. (2005). *National Reconstruction and Poverty Reduction - the Role of Women in Afghanistan's Future.* Washington, DC: World Bank.

The World Fact Book. (2005). *Afghanistan.* Washington, D.C.: Central Intelligence Agency.

Thompson, J. B. (1995). *The Media and Modernity.* Cambridge: Polity.

Tilly, C. (2002). *Stories, Identities and Political Change.* New York: Rowman & Littlefield.

United Nations Assistance Mission to Afghanistan (UNAMA). (2001). The Bonn Agreement. Retrieved December 5, 2005, from www.unama-afg.org/docs/bonn/bonn.html

United Nations Development Fund for Women (UNIFEM). (2004). *Gender Profile of the Conflict in Afghanistan.* New York: United Nations.

United Nations Development Programme (UNDP). (2002). *Afghanistan: Preliminary Needs Assessment for Recovery and Reconstruction.* Geneva: United Nations Development Programme

United Nations Development Programme (UNDP), & Islamic Republic of Afghanistan. (2004). *Security with a Human Face: Challenges and Responsibilities.* Kabul: UNDP.

World Press Encyclopedia. (2003). Afghanistan. In A. Quick (Ed.), *World Press Encyclopedia* (Vol. 1; A - M, pp. 1-4). New York City: Thomson - Gale.

Young, I. M. (1996). Communication and the Other: Beyond Deliberative Democracy. In S. Benhabib (Ed.), *Democracy and Difference: Contesting the boundaries of the political* (pp. 120-137). Princeton: Princeton University Press.

Young, I. M. (2003). Activist Challenges to Deliberative Democracy. In J. Fishkin & P. Laslett (Eds.), *Debating Deliberative Democracy* (pp. 102-120). Malden: Blackwell Publishing.

Zakaria, F. (2003). *The Future of Freedom: Illiberal Democracy at Home and Abroad.* New York: W. W. Norton & Company, Inc.

1375341R0

Printed in Great Britain by
Amazon.co.uk, Ltd.,
Marston Gate.